L O T H I A N   G A R D E N   S E R I E S

HYDROPONIC GARDENING

Acknowledgements

The author and publisher acknowledge and
thank Howard M. Resh, the author of
Hydroponic Food Production (Woodbridge
Press, 1990), and publisher for permission
to use the following line drawings based on
illustrations in that book: pages 18, 22, 24,
27, 28, 34, 35, 42.

Thomas C. Lothian Pty Ltd
11 Munro Street,
Port Melbourne, Victoria 3207

Copyright © Steven Carruthers 1993
Copyright © illustrations Thomas C. Lothian
    Pty Ltd 1993

First published 1993
Reprinted 1994, 1996, 1997

National Library of Australia
Cataloguing-in-publication data:

Carruthers, Steven L., 1951 –
Hydroponic gardening.

Includes index.
ISBN 0 85091 557 0.

1. Hydroponics. 2. Gardening.
3. Gardening – Australia. I. Title.
(Series: Lothian garden series.)

631.585

Cover design by David Constable
Illustrations by Julia McLeish
Photography by Steven Carruthers
Typeset in Cheltenham and Rockwell by
    Bookset Pty Ltd
Printed by PT Pac-Rim Kwartanusa Printing,
    Indonesia

Foreword

Hydroponics might be seen by some as a recent fad, or a novelty to be pursued by those with plenty of time and space. Far from it, as Steven Carruthers shows in this addition to the Lothian Australian gardening series, hydroponics is not a recent gimmick but an age-old approach to plant cultivation. It can also be an efficient way of growing plants as you may have fewer problems with pests and disease and plant growth may be speedier because the plants receive a constant supply of nutrients that they can readily use.

Not all of us will want to convert our back garden to the cultivation of plants by hydroponics but we may enjoy experimenting with some of the smaller systems available. And those with balconies rather than backyards may find hydroponics the simplest and most effective way to grow a few herbs, vegetables or flowers. The use of hydroponic planter systems also allows effective, continuous supply of water during the heat of our summers, a time when plants in containers are easily stressed.

Whether you seek an ambitious hydroponics scheme or simply an answer to growing a few pots on your balcony, this book should help you by providing practical advice and answers to your questions, easy or difficult, to extend your success as a hydroponics gardener.

JOHN PATRICK
Series Editor

Contents

Introduction

Hydroponics, the science of growing plants without soil, is one of the most interesting advances in modern horticulture. The natural elements necessary for plant growth are used to produce luxurious, healthy plants that are free of weeds and soil-borne pests and diseases.

Also known as soilless culture, hydroponic growing techniques have been used for centuries. The earliest recorded references date back to the hanging gardens of Babylon and the floating gardens of Kashmir, and to the Aztec Indians of Mexico who grew plants on rafts in shallow lakes. A few of these rafts can still be found today on the lakes near Mexico City. Egyptian hieroglyphic records dating back to several hundred years B.C. also describe the growing of plants in water. In modern times, mobile hydroponic farms were used to feed GIs throughout their long campaign in the South Pacific during the Second World War, and to feed the occupation forces in Japan after the war.

Today, hydroponics is playing an increasingly important role in the world's agricultural development. Population pressures, climatic changes, soil erosion, inequitable water distribution and polluted ground water are all factors which are influencing alternative horticultural methods. Since its recent revival, hydroponics is being adapted to many situations, from outdoor field culture and indoor greenhouse culture to a highly specialised application in nuclear submarines which provides fresh vegetables for crews. It is a space-age science, but at the same time it is being used in developing countries of the Third World to provide intensive food production in limited areas. Its only restraints are sources of fresh water and nutrients. In areas where fresh water is not available, hydroponics can use seawater that has been desalinated.

In Australia, where climatic conditions are harsh and unpredictable and arable land is limited, hydroponics is used to meet urban market demands for fresh produce and fresh cut flowers for local and export markets, and to grow fodder for livestock during winter and in drought-stricken regions. For the home gardener, it is an economical and simple way to turn pocket-handkerchief-sized backyards into productive vegetable and flower gardens.

The future of hydroponics is assured, with plans now in place to establish a permanent space-station colony and a colony on the moon within our lifetime. Research by NASA is bringing us closer to achieving that, and is revealing a great deal about plants along the way.

Hydroponics is simply a highly efficient way to provide food and water to plants. In a soil garden, food and water are randomly distributed and plants need to expend a lot of energy growing roots to find them. In a hydroponic garden, the food and water are delivered directly to the plants' roots. The

Hanging gardens of Babylon.

plants grow faster and can be harvested sooner because they are putting their energy into growing above the ground, not under it.

Once established, plants flourish, giving higher-than-average yields, even on balconies and in small backyard areas. Plants can be grown closer together than in normal gardens because they do not have to compete with weeds and other plants for water and available nutrients.

Contrary to popular belief, there is no physiological difference between plants grown hydroponically and those grown in soil.

The subsequent process of mineral (and water) uptake by the plants is the same for both growing environments. The fundamental difference is in the way in which the nutrients are delivered to the plants.

In soil the nutrient salts necessary for healthy growth are contained in organic matter, and might not be released as and when required by the plant. Soil gardens are fertilised with manures and composts made of decayed organic matter; but plants cannot use this matter until it has broken down into the basic nutrient salts — a slow process.

In hydroponics, the nutrient salts are already refined and purified (in much the same way as sugar is refined from cane), and are immediately available to the plants. As a result, flowering and fruiting are achieved thirty to forty per cent sooner than in soil.

While hydroponics has been applied commercially since the early 1970s, only recently has it become popular among home gardeners. Pressures on the size of urban blocks of land and spiralling vegetable prices are largely responsible for this growing demand. Consumers are also becoming more aware of the environment they live in. Soil degradation, deforestation, chemical pesticides and food additives are all of concern, making consumers more vocal in their demand for environmentally friendly products and produce.

Commercially, hydroponics tends to go hand in hand with artificial lighting. This is primarily so that commercial growers can bring their crops to market out of season and on time; for example, so that chrysanthemums are available on Mother's Day. However, for the home gardener, the principles of growing plants under artificial lights can be complex and the set-up and running costs can be prohibitive. Additionally, different plants require different lighting schedules to obtain the best results. If you wish to grow plants indoors, you should refer to books specifically addressing this subject. Meanwhile, this book assumes that sunlight is available to the hydroponic gardener.

While the idea of hydroponics might still intimidate some people, most gardeners readily embrace this simple, quick and easy process. It is certainly no more complicated than traditional gardening methods, and exactly the same horticultural principles apply to both. Although a small degree of technology is involved, one should not be daunted by it. This book, I trust, will inform and inspire the budding hydroponic gardener and help to extend the repertoire of gardeners who have already started on this exciting road.

Advantages of hydroponics

The main advantage of soilless culture over soil culture is increased yield. Although the difference is greater when soil conditions are poor, higher yields from hydroponics are mainly due to a more efficient use of water and fertilisers. For crops whose yields are comparable, such as strawberries, the quality of hydroponically grown fruit is much higher than that grown in soil. Other advantages of hydroponics are as follows:

- Slightly denser planting is possible.
- Produce looks better.
- Produce lasts longer.
- Less water is used.
- Water stress in hot conditions is reduced.
- It is suited to non-arable areas.
- Plants do not need to search or compete for available nutrients as they do in soil.
- Plants reach maturity in a much shorter time because the nutrients they receive are balanced and ready to use.
- Soil pests and diseases are considerably reduced.
- Hydroponic gardens require less maintenance because there are no weeds to remove.

Disadvantages of hydroponics

The initial capital costs of setting up a hydroponic garden can be high. However, simple, low-cost hydroponic systems can be improvised using odds and ends which can nearly always be found around the home. The other main disadvantages of hydroponics are diseases, which can spread rapidly through a system, and nutritional problems, which can occur from time to time. Both of these can be overcome or prevented by a good management programme.

Plant nutrition

Modern-day hydroponics has evolved from early studies of plant constituents, which led to the discovery of essential plant elements. Plant nutrition is therefore the basis of hydroponics. Anyone intending to adopt soilless culture techniques should have a good knowledge of this subject, as management of plant nutrition through management of the nutrient solution is the key to success in hydroponic gardening.

The hydroponic method enables gardeners to control available nutrients. In conventional gardening, once fertilisers or nutrients are added to soil there is no easy way to change or reduce their concentrations. In hydroponics, by contrast, the nutrient solution can be adjusted or changed to suit the particular stage of plant growth. Also, not needing to search or compete for available nutrients as they do in soil, the plants reach maturity much sooner because the nutrients provided are already balanced and ready to use. In simple terms, optimisation of plant nutrition is more easily achieved in hydroponics than in soil.

Elements

Elements are listed in several groups or classifications, depending upon the amount normally used by plants in their growth and development.

Macro-elements

Nitrogen	(N)
Phosphorus	(P)
Potassium	(K)

Secondary macro-elements

Calcium	(Ca)
Magnesium	(Mg)
Sulphur	(S)

Micro-elements

Iron	(Fe)
Boron	(Bo)
Zinc	(Zn)
Copper	(Cu)
Manganese	(Mn)
Molybdenum	(Mo)
Chlorine	(Cl)

Basic elements

While ninety-two natural mineral elements are known to exist, only sixty of these have been found in plants. Of these sixty, only sixteen are considered essential for plant growth.

To be considered essential for healthy plant growth, an element must fulfil four criteria:

- It must be necessary for the plant to complete its life cycle.
- Its action must be specific (that is, not wholly replaceable by any other element).
- It must be directly involved in the nutrition of the plant (that is, required for the action of an essential enzyme).
- It must not antagonise a toxic effect of another element.

The sixteen elements that are generally considered essential for plant growth are divided into macro-elements (those that are required in relatively large quantities) and micro-elements or trace elements (those needed in considerably smaller quantities).

The macro-elements are carbon (C), hydrogen (H), oxygen (O), nitrogen (N), phosphorus (P), potassium (K), calcium (Ca), magnesium (Mg) and sulphur (S). The micro-elements are iron (Fe), chlorine (Cl), boron (B), manganese (Mn), copper (Cu), zinc (Zn) and molybdenum (Mo).

Essential elements and what they do

Macro-elements

Carbon (C) is a constituent found in all organic compounds.

Hydrogen (H) is a constituent of all organic compounds of which carbon is a constituent. It is important for the cation exchange in plant–medium relations.

Oxygen (O) is a constituent of many organic compounds. It is essential in the anion exchange between roots and the external medium.

Nitrogen (N) is used in various forms to promote rapid vegetative growth, leaf, flower, fruit and seed development, and chlorophyll development; and to increase the protein content in all plants.

Phosphorus (P) promotes and stimulates early growth and blooming and root growth. It hastens maturity and seed growth, and it contributes to the general hardiness of plants.

Potassium (K) promotes disease resistance and good development of carbohydrates, starches and sugars, and it increases fruit production.

Hydroponics
A technique for intensive horticulture involving the growing of plants in systems isolated from the soil, either with or without a medium, and fed with the total water and nutrients that the plants require. This term is in general use only in Australia, New Zealand and the USA. The term used worldwide is *soilless culture*. The term *hydroponics* which can be misleading is sometimes used to indicate water-based systems in contrast to media-based systems. This book uses both terms to mean the same.

Availability of nutrient elements

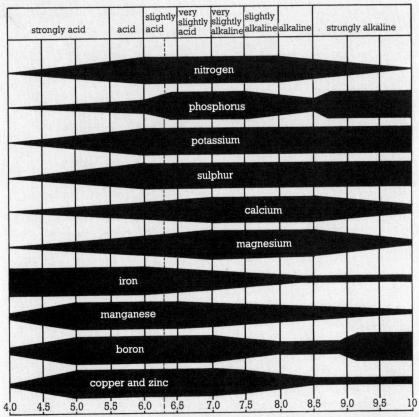

Nutrient deficiencies will become apparent if the pH is higher or lower than the recommended pH range for individual plants. For example, if your pH is consistently 7.5, you can expect interveinal chlorosis to occur, an indication of an iron deficiency.

The chart shows a pH range of 4.0 to 10.0. The width of the black section for each nutrient represents the maximum availability of that nutrient. The widest place denotes the most availability. The narrowest place denotes the least availability. The dotted line at 6.25 indicates the maximum number of elements at their highest availability.

Organic and inorganic solutions

Hydroponics and organics might seem to be odd bedfellows. In the past, devotees of each have tended to regard one another with a certain degree of suspicion, believing that their respective practices were somehow opposed. But there *is* common ground, and this is proving to be an area of great interest to many new and prospective hydroponic growers. Organic products are natural or are made from a combination of natural products. For gardeners who are detractors from inorganic formulations, there are many organic nutrients specifically designed for hydroponics. Among the more popular are formulations containing earthworm castings, seabird and bat guano, and sea kelp. These nutrients are widely available in powdered, granulated or water soluble form, and give excellent results when used alone or as additives to inorganic fertilisers. When using organic products for growing plants, the grower is trying to work *with* nature, not against it. Also, organic formulations are known to build the immune system of plants, helping to guard against pests and diseases.

Calcium (Ca) is vital in all parts of plants to promote the translocation of carbohydrates, healthy cell wall structure, strong stems, membrane maintenance and root structure development. It sometimes interferes with the ability of magnesium to activate enzymes.

Magnesium (Mg) promotes the absorption and translocation of phosphorus. It activates many enzymes and it appears to aid in the formation of oils and fats. It also plays a role in carbon dioxide assimilation.

Sulphur (S) promotes the synthesis of oils, good cell wall structure, and the synthesis and function of protein.

Micro-elements

Iron (Fe) acts as a catalyst in the photosynthesis and respiration process, and it is essential for the formation of sugars and starches. Iron also activates certain other enzymes.

Chlorine (Cl) is essential for photosynthesis where it acts as an enzyme activator during the production of oxygen from water.

Boron (B) is not well understood, but it might aid carbohydrate transport.

Manganese (Mn) activates one or more enzymes in fatty acid synthesis and the enzymes responsible for DNA and RNA formation. It also participates directly in the photosynthetic production of oxygen from water and may be involved in chlorophyll formation. Manganese is closely associated with copper and zinc.

Copper (Cu) is an internal catalyst and acts as an electron carrier. It is also thought to be involved in nitrogen fixation.

Zinc (Zn), with copper and manganese, is linked to chlorophyll synthesis. It is also essential for auxin metabolism.

Molybdenum (Mo) acts as an electron carrier in the conversion of nitrate to ammonium. It is essential for nitrogen fixation and nitrate reduction.

Nutrient solutions

For hydroponic applications, all essential elements are supplied to plants in the form of nutrient solution, which consists of fertiliser salts dissolved in water. While many commercial growers formulate their own nutrient solution for a particular crop, the home gardener can choose from a range of good-quality hydroponic solutions already formulated and packaged in small containers. Many of these formulations are exactly the same as those used by commercial growers.

While it is not necessary in this book to delve deeply into nutrient formulations, it can be fairly stated that these take much of the guesswork out of plant nutrition for the home gardener.

It is important to avoid any pre-packed, concentrated nutrient solution that contains sludge. Nutrient salts have different solubilities — that is, different concentrations of salt that will remain in solution when dissolved with water. If a fertiliser salt has a low solubility, only a small amount will dissolve in water. In hydroponics, fertiliser salts must have high solubilities since they must remain in solution in order to be available to the plants. The presence of sludge in pre-packed liquid nutrients, or lack of solubility when powdered formulations are mixed with water, is an indication of poor-grade nutrient salts. The sludge contains inert carriers, such as clay, silt and sand particles, which do not supply ions. Such impurities can block the availability of other nutrients to plant roots, as well as blocking feeder lines.

Most nutrient solutions available on the market contain all the essential elements for plant growth, and are classified as general purpose solutions.

The best of these solutions are considered suitable for almost any system, with the exception of rockwool which is more alkaline than other mediums and so requires a different nutrient profile.

Nutrient formulations are available in either powder or liquid form. While each has its followers, liquid nutrient is more popular among home gardeners because of its consistency and its easy and convenient mixing instructions.

Nutrient is also available in a 'grow' and a 'bloom' formulation so that plants can utilise different elements at different stages of their growing cycles. In the early stages they need more nitrogen for the production of leaves, shoots and stems. This is called the 'vegetative' stage of growth. As plants mature, they begin to set buds, a sign that they are entering a reproductive phase. At this time plants will begin to use less nitrogen and more potassium and phosphorus, the elements associated with the formation of flowers and fruit. The change from a 'grow' to a 'bloom' formulation helps a plant to maximise its potential to set flowers and fruit.

Some very good one-part nutrients are also available which use high-quality components known as chelates (pronounced 'key-lates'). These nutrients are suitable for a wide range of plants and systems and are easy to use.

Replacing the solution

Individual plants absorb elements at varying rates and in varying quantities. As a result, some elements become in short supply before others. The exact deficiency of individual elements in the solution used in hydroponics is impossible to determine without costly laboratory analyses. The only safeguard against nutrient disorders is therefore to replace the solution regularly.

In any hydroponic system where the nutrient solution is recycled, which is the majority of cases, the life of the solution is two to three weeks, depending upon the season, the nature of the crop and the stage of plant growth. During the hot summer months, when plants transpire more, take up more water and therefore the nutrients concentrate, the nutrient solution might have to be changed as often as once a week, especially if plants have reached an advanced stage of growth.

Nutrient management

While optimum nutrition is easy to achieve in hydroponics, so is damage to plants due to errors in making up the nutrient solution and/or failure to adjust it daily. In systems that are controlled to any degree by automatic devices, poor maintenance and equipment failure can also damage or destroy plants.

The success or failure of a hydroponic garden therefore depends primarily on a strict nutrient management programme, and this is achieved by carefully manipulating the pH level, temperature and electroconductivity of the solution. This manipulation, combined with a rudimentary knowledge of both, is the key to successful hydroponic gardening.

pH level

In simple terms, pH is a measure of acidity or alkalinity on a scale of 1 to 14. In a nutrient solution, the pH level determines the availability of essential plant elements. A solution is deemed to be neutral at pH 7.0, alkaline if above and acidic if below.

In soil, most plants prefer a pH level on the acidic side of neutral. Most hydroponically grown plants prefer a slightly more acidic solution, with the

As a general rule, plants have a higher nutrient requirement during cooler months, and a lower requirement in the hotter months. A stronger nutrient solution should therefore be maintained during winter, with a weaker solution during summer, when plants take up and transpire more water than nutrient.

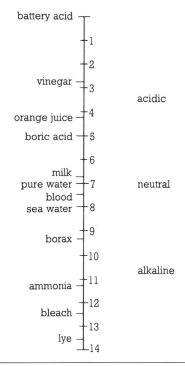

pH values for commonly used liquids.

Effects of pH

A high pH can reduce the availability of iron, manganese, boron, copper, zinc and phosphorus to plants. A low pH can reduce the availability of potassium, sulphur, calcium, magnesium and phosphorus.

Nutrients and light

Low light conditions cause plants to take up more potassium and phosphorus, thereby making the nutrient solution more acidic. This is particularly evident on overcast days. Conversely, on clear sunny days, plants take up more nitrogen, making the nutrient solution more alkaline.

EC (electrical conductivity)

An indicator of the strength of a nutrient solution, as measured by an EC meter. This is the preferred term used worldwide. Its most common unit is milliSiemens per centimetre (mS/cm). Another unit is microSiemens per centimetre (μS/cm). A limitation of EC is that it indicates only the total concentration of a solution and not the individual nutrient components.

optimum pH being between 5.8 and 6.5. For pH values above 7.5, iron, manganese, copper, zinc and boron become less available to plants. Should the pH of a nutrient solution fall below pH 6.0, then the solubility of phosphoric acid, calcium and manganese drops sharply. While hydroponic crops can be grown successfully at higher and lower levels, the further one departs from the recommended range the greater the odds against success.

Whereas the degree of acidity or alkalinity in soil is controlled by adding either lime or dolomite, the pH range of nutrient solution can be controlled by chemical buffers when it strays outside the ideal. It can be lowered by adding dilute concentrations of phosphoric or nitric acid and raised by adding a dilute concentration of potassium hydroxide.

In hydroponics the movement of the pH balance gives a good indication of plant activity. If the pH is rising, or the solution is becoming more alkaline, then the plant is taking acidic nutrient salts out of the solution, which can cause toxic salt build-up and limit water intake. Conversely, if the pH is falling or becoming more acidic, then the plant is taking up alkaline components, which can make the nutrient chemically bound by acid salts and the plant roots are unable to absorb it.

As a general rule, the pH of a nutrient solution should be tested daily with simple water-testing kits or inexpensive electronic testers and the solution should be adjusted, if necessary, by using acid or alkaline buffers.

Always perform this check at the same time of day and, if possible, at the same temperature because the pH of a solution can fluctuate dramatically with light and temperature variations during the course of the day. Intense photosynthetic activity during daylight hours causes the pH to rise and at dusk, when photosynthesis ceases, intense plant respiration causes the pH to drop. Adding buffers to even out these short-term changes can put your system on a roller coaster that is harmful to the plants. Although it is important to stay within the recommended pH range, it is far more important to prevent large fluctuations.

Temperature

Temperature fluctuations in a hydroponic solution can affect not only the pH but also the solubility of nutrients. Studies have shown that the ideal water temperature for total solubility is between 20°C and 22°C. If the water temperature falls outside this range, then many trace elements become insoluble. While most plants can survive outside this range, plant health and yield are severely affected.

Temperatures higher and lower than the ideal affect plants in the same way as extremes of pH.

Electroconductivity

During growth, plants take up the elements they require, thereby altering the balance of the remaining nutrient solution from day to day. This feeding process is termed electroconductivity. To determine the general extent of nutrient uptake, the remaining solution should be tested daily and adjusted if required.

If high concentrations of nutrients are revealed, this is an indication that the plants are taking up water faster than they are taking up essential elements. It follows that, as water is removed by plants, the volume of the solution decreases, with a subsequent increase in nutrient strength, which might harm the plants. In this situation, fresh water should be added to the nutrient solution until the optimum concentration level is reached.

Conversely, for lower-than-normal nutrient concentrations, plants are taking up more nutrients than water and the solution needs to be adjusted with additional nutrients.

There are several simple and inexpensive electronic meters which allow the home gardener to measure easily and quickly the electroconductivity (EC) or the total dissolved salts (TDS) or conductivity factor (cF), as it is also known. These instruments use a variety of scales, with the strength of nutrient solutions expressed as either parts per million (ppm), for TDS meters, or milliSiemens (mS) for EC meters. To convert milliSiemens to conductivity factors, multiply by 10. To convert conductivity factors to parts per million, multiply by 70. For optimum results, a meter that will measure nutrient strength is indispensable not only to the commercial grower but also to the serious home gardener. If a meter is not available the nutrient solution should be discarded weekly, and a fresh solution made.

Plant requirements

Plants can be categorised generally as either low, medium or heavy feeders, and require correspondingly low, medium or high nutrient strengths. Only plants that fall into one category should be grown together using the same nutrient strength. To do otherwise will give only one plant type the optimum growing conditions, making the others slower to mature.

Any plants grown outside the optimum EC or TDS range will result in poor-quality fruit and flowers. For example, a high-strength solution will make a low feeder, such as lettuce, taste bitter and a low-strength nutrient solution will make medium feeders, such as strawberries, and high feeders such as tomatoes, tasteless, soft and squashy.

During the early development of hydroponics in Australia, when there was less data available on plant nutrition, hydroponically grown fruit and vegetables earned a reputation for being tasteless. Today, hydroponic produce is full of flavour. Should your produce lack taste and vigour, you can safely assume that it has been grown outside the optimum nutrient range. For optimum EC or TDS ranges for various plants, consult the Nutrient guide on page 12.

Conversion chart		
mS/cm	cF	ppm
0.5	5	350
1.0	10	700
1.5	15	1050
2.0	20	1400
2.5	25	1750
3.0	30	2100
3.5	35	2450
4.0	40	2800
4.5	45	3150
5.0	50	3500

Nutrient strength

For most plants the total concentration of nutrient elements in a solution should be between 500 and 1500 ppm so that osmotic pressure will facilitate absorption. However, some, such as tomatoes, need a nutrient concentration as high as 3500 ppm. Lower values are preferred by low-feeding crops such as watercress. The middle values are preferred by medium-feeding crops such as cucumbers.

A sample of water should be taken daily and tested for pH and electroconductivity. Not all plants share the same electroconductivity and therefore plants should be grown together according to their mean nutrient requirement. Plants will tolerate a wide pH range and, generally, if the electroconductivity is right, the pH will follow.

Potatoes grown in an aggregate drip-irrigation system.

As a general rule, plants will have a higher nutrient requirement during the cooler months and a lower requirement in the hotter months. Therefore, a stronger nutrient solution should be maintained during winter, with a weaker solution during summer when the plants take up and transpire more water than nutrients.

Telegraph cucumbers grown in polystyrene boxes filled with perlite and fed by trickle irrigation.

Nutrient guide

Fruit	pH	Electro-conductivity	cF	ppm
Banana	5.5–6.5	M	18–22	1260–1540
Black currant	6.0	L	14–18	980–1260
Blueberry	4.0–5.0	M	18–20	1260–1400
Melon	5.5–6.0	H	20–25	1400–1750
Passionfruit	6.5	M	16–24	840–1680
Paw paw	6.5	H	20–24	1400–1680
Pineapple	5.5–6.0	H	20–24	1400–1680
Red currant	6.0	M	14–18	980–1260
Rhubarb	5.5–6.0	M	16–20	840–1400
Strawberries	6.0	M	18–22	1260–1540
Watermelon	5.8	M	18–24	1260–1680

Vegetables				
Artichoke	6.5–7.5	L	8–18	560–1260
Asparagus	6.0–6.8	L	14–18	980–1260
Bean (common)	6.0	H	20–40	1400–2800
Beetroot	6.0–6.5	H	18–50	1260–3500
Broad bean	6.0–6.5	M	18–22	1260–1540
Broccoli	6.0–6.8	H	28–35	1960–2450
Brussel sprout	6.5	H	25–30	1750–2100
Cabbage	6.5–7.0	H	25–30	1750–2100
Capsicum	6.0–6.5	M	18–22	1260–1540
Carrot	6.3	M	16–20	1120–1400
Cauliflower	6.5–7.0	M	15–20	1050–1400
Celery	6.5	M	18–24	1260–1680
Cucumber	5.5	M	17–25	1190–1750
Eggplant	6.0	H	25–35	1750–2450
Endive	5.5	M	20–24	1400–1680
Fodder	6.0	M	18–20	1260–1400
Garlic	6.0	L	14–18	980–1260
Leek	6.5–7.0	L	14–18	980–1260
Lettuce	6.0–7.0	L	8–12	560–840
Marrow	6.0	M	18–24	1260–1680
Okra	6.5	H	20–24	1400–1680
Onions	6.0–6.7	L	14–18	980–1260
Pak-choi	7.0	M	15–20	1050–1400
Parsnip	6.0	L	14–18	980–1260
Pea	6.0–7.0	L	8–18	980–1260
Pepino	6.0–6.5	H	20–50	1400–3500
Potato	5.0–6.0	H	20–25	1400–1750
Pumpkin	5.5–7.5	M	18–24	1260–1680
Radish	6.0–7.0	M	16–22	840–1540
Spinach	6.0–7.0	M	18–23	1260–1610
Silverbeet	6.0–7.0	M	18–23	1260–1610
Sweet corn	6.0	M	16–24	840–1680
Sweet potato	5.5–6.0	H	20–25	1400–1750
Taro	5.0–5.5	H	25–30	1750–2100
Tomato	6.0–6.5	H	20–50	1400–3500
Turnip	6.0–6.5	M	18–24	1260–1680
Zucchini	6.0	M	18–24	1260–1680

	pH	Electro-conductivity	cF	ppm
Herbs				
Basil	5.5–6.0	L	10–16	700–1120
Chicory	5.5–6.0	H	20–24	1400–1680
Chives	6.0–6.5	M	18–22	1260–1540
Fennel	6.4–6.8	L	10–14	700–980
Lavender	6.4–6.8	L	10–14	700–980
Lemon balm	5.5–6.5	L	10–16	700–1120
Marjoram	6.0	M	16–20	1120–1400
Mint	5.5–6.0	H	20–24	1400–1680
Mustard cress	6.0–6.5	M	12–24	840–1680
Parsley	5.5–6.0	L	8–18	560–1260
Rosemary	5.5–6.0	L	10–16	700–1120
Sage	5.5–6.5	L	10–16	700–1120
Thyme	5.5–7.0	L	8–16	560–1120
Watercress	6.5–6.8	L	4–18	280–1260
Flowers				
African Violet	6.0–7.0	L	12–15	840–1050
Anthurium	5.0–6.0	M	16–20	1120–1400
Antirrhinum	6.5	M	16–20	1120–1400
Aphelandra	5.0–6.0	M	18–24	1260–1680
Aster	6.0–6.5	M	18–24	1260–1680
Begonia	6.5	L	14–18	980–1260
Bromeliad	5.0–7.5	L	8–12	560–840
Caladium	6.0–7.5	M	16–20	1120–1400
Canna	6.0	M	18–24	1260–1680
Carnation	6.0	H	20–35	1400–2450
Chrysanthemum	6.0–6.2	M	18–25	1400–1750
Cymbidium	5.5	L	6–10	420–560
Dahlia	6.0–7.0	M	15–20	1050–1400
Dieffenbachia	5.0–6.0	M	18–24	1400–1680
Dracaena	5.0–6.0	M	18–24	1400–1680
Fern	6.0	M	16–20	1120–1400
Ficus	5.5–6.0	M	16–24	1120–1680
Freesia	6.5	M	10–20	700–1400
Impatiens	5.5–6.5	M	18–20	1260–1400
Gerbera	5.0–6.5	M	20–25	1400–1750
Gladiolus	5.5–6.5	M	20–24	1400–1680
Monstera	5.0–6.0	M	18–24	1400–1680
Palm	6.0–7.5	M	16–20	1120–1400
Rose	5.5–6.0	M	15–25	1050–1750
Stock	6.0–7.0	M	16–20	1120–1400

Low (L)	Medium (M)	High (H)
0.6–1.5 mS/cm	1.5–2.4 mS/cm	2.4–5.0mS/cm

NOTE: The pH and electroconductivity values specified here are given as a broad range. It should be noted that specific plant requirements will vary according to regional climatic conditions, and from season to season.

Know your crop

Plant EC or cF can vary according to the stage of growth. For example, cucumbers prefer cF 20 when establishing, and cF 25 after the first harvest. Between 3 and 7 weeks after first harvest, the optimum cF is 17.

For easy growing reference, plants that share broad groupings of low, medium or high nutrient electroconductivity can be grown together, providing that a middle-ground nutrient strength is adopted.

Carnations grown in a rockwool drip-irrigation system.

Rhubarb grown in an aggregate drip-irrigation system.

Hydroponic mediums and techniques

Recirculating systems

Systems in which the bulk of nutrient solution that has been used is recycled and re-used numerous times. These are also known as 'closed' systems. Different systems can be either run continuously, as with NFT, or intermittently, as with the flood-and-drain technique. Currently, less than ten per cent of the world's commercial hydroponic production uses these types of systems.

Non-recirculating systems

Medium systems in which the system is fed with fresh nutrient solution to replace what the plant has used, with a slight excess displaced which is not recycled into the system. Also known as 'open' or 'run-to-waste' systems. Over ninety per cent of the world's commercial hydroponic production uses these types of systems.

Aeroponics

A system in which the roots of a plant are continuously or intermittently in an environment saturated with fine drops (a mist or aerosol) of nutrient solution.

One of the first steps in establishing a hydroponic system is to choose a growing medium. There are several options, and it is worth examining their relative merits.

Many growers find that mixes of different mediums work well for them, though finding the right combination might be a question of trial and error. Most importantly, you should know the characteristics of a medium before buying it and ensure that it suits the type of hydroponic system you are using.

The medium, or 'substrate' used in soilless culture is more than simply a means of support for plants. For optimum results it must also provide oxygen, hold water effectively and offer perfect drainage. The type of medium used determines the method of nutrient application: if the medium can draw liquid upwards by capillary action, then the nutrient solution is applied from underneath. Mediums that do not have this capillary capacity but are used because of other advantages require watering by surface methods such as trickle, drip or spray.

Essentially, hydroponic mediums need to be 'inert substrates' — neither contributing nor altering nutrients, and thereby giving the grower complete nutritional control. Hydroponic systems are broadly grouped, according to the type of medium used, into water culture (NFT), aggregate culture, rockwool culture, sawdust culture and aeroponics. Aggregates include a broad range of alternative materials: crushed granite, broken rocks, coal cinders, crushed corals, volcanic cinders and broken bricks, in addition to the more

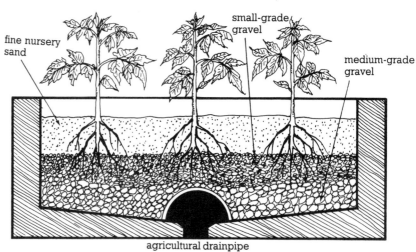

A cross-section of plants growing in a combined gravel and sand mixture.

popular types such as vermiculite, perlite and expanded clay. The choice between these will be dictated, to an extent, by factors such as availability, cost, climate and system type.

The moisture retention of a medium is one of the most important characteristics and is influenced by the size, shape and porosity of the particles. Water is retained on the surface of the particles and within the pore space. The more porous the material, the greater the quantity of water that can be stored within the particles themselves and thus the higher the water retention of the medium. Smaller particles are more water retentive than large ones because they have proportionately greater surface area and pore space, and they pack together more tightly.

But the moisture-retention factor is only half of the equation. Drainage must also be considered, and indeed a highly retentive medium will be of use only if it can also drain freely. This allows for adequate aeration and oxygen movement around the root zone. Because a balance of water and air is needed in the root medium, growers often find that a mixture of different mediums gives the best result — for example, two aggregates of different sizes. After watering, 10 to 20 per cent of the volume of a root medium should be occupied by air and 35 to 50 per cent by water.

Another, more technical, characteristic of suitable hydroponic mediums is the 'cation exchange capacity' (CEC). Cations are particles which have a positive charge, and many important plant nutrients (for example, potassium, calcium, magnesium and iron) occur in the nutrient solution as cations. These nutrient particles attach themselves to medium particles which have a negative charge, thereby staying in the medium and not quickly leaching away. As a result, they are available to the plant roots for longer. Mediums that attract a large number of cations are described as having a high CEC — a desirable characteristic. Clearly, hydroponic mediums with a high CEC require less-frequent application of nutrients than those with a low CEC. Peat moss and vermiculite are examples of mediums with a high CEC, while sand, perlite, and polystyrene have low CEC ratings.

Hydroponic mediums must be free of all toxic materials and salt and should not influence the pH of the nutrient solution. They also need to be durable, so that they don't disintegrate or lose their structure; this would lead to compaction and hence poor root aeration.

Periodic sterilisation of the medium is a good idea, as pests and diseases build up in the system over a period of time. Sterilisation is done by steam or chemicals, the former method being the more economical. Chemicals used for sterilisation may be gases, such as methyl bromide and chloropicrin, or liquids, such as formaldehyde and chlorine. These chemicals are broad spectrum, killing a range of insects, nematodes and fungi. Obviously, where chemicals are used there will be a delay before beds can be planted again. In some cases a thorough flushing with water is necessary before planting.

Cation exchange

The ability of an absorbing material such as root medium to hold various nutrients, including ammonium-nitrogen, potassium, calcium, magnesium, iron, manganese, zinc and copper. A root medium with low cation exchange capacity does not retain nutrients well and so must be fertilised often.

NFT system

Water culture

In typical nutrient film technique (NFT) systems, plants are grown in channels so that roots are bathed to a depth of about 2 mm in a thin film of continuously flowing nutrient solution. NFT systems are usually of the recirculating type. The nutrient solution flows past the plant roots, then drains back to the nutrient reservoir where it is recirculated with a pump.

The NFT system was originally designed and developed by Dr Allen Cooper of Sussex, England. It is officially described by the International Society for Soilless Culture (ISOSC) as a system in which 'a very shallow stream of water containing all the dissolved nutrients required for growth is recircu-

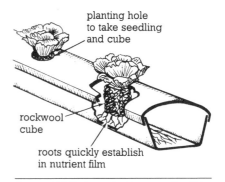

planting hole to take seedling and cube

rockwool cube

roots quickly establish in nutrient film

A typical NFT channel with removable lid. The nutrient solution drains into a collector.

NFT (nutrient film technique)
A water-based system in which nutrient solution flows down channels or gullies and is recirculated. A basic principle of the technique is that the nutrient solution should be maintained as a thin film to enable adequate oxygenation of the solution.

lated past the bare roots of crop plants in a watertight gully'. The ISOSC makes the following recommendations: 'Ideally, the depth of the recirculatory stream should be very shallow, little more than a film of water — hence the name nutrient film. This ensures that the thick root mat, which develops in the bottom of the gully, has an upper surface which, although moist, is in the air. Consequently, there is an abundant supply of oxygen to the roots of the plants.

Since their development, NFT systems have changed little in design. However, to get the best results, some understanding is required of the needs of different crops.

For example, plants such as lettuce only require a low concentration of nutrient solution for optimum growth, and because of their small root structure they are ideally suited to NFT systems. However, tomato plants require a stronger nutrient solution and a larger channel size in order to accommodate their large root structure. Plants with a large root structure may restrict the flow of nutrients through the channel once they reach maturity.

NFT systems are used to grow lettuce, tomatoes, endive, cucumbers, zucchini, peppers, strawberries, silverbeet, parsley and many other leafy vegetables and herbs. They are not suitable for growing root or tuber crops.

The main advantage of the NFT system is that plant roots are automatically exposed to adequate supplies of water, oxygen and nutrients. In other types of systems, an imbalance of one of these three can result in an imbalance of one or both of the others. Because of its design, NFT can meet all three requirements at the same time, producing high yields and high-quality crops from high-density planting.

The disadvantage of NFT is the risk of flooding, waterlogged roots, or other problems due to poor design, construction or operation which can cause crop losses. These problems can be avoided if growers follow the simple principles of NFT systems outlined above. Other disadvantages are associated with the dependence of NFT on reliable supplies of water and power. If a breakdown occurs, and suitable back-ups do not exist, the grower can suffer more serious losses than in systems with a degree of buffering.

Aggregate culture

Sand

Sand is probably the oldest hydroponic medium known. However, not all are alike and not all are suitable for use in a hydroponic system. Granitic or silica-type sands should be used, not calcareous sands, which are too alkaline. Beach sand is generally unsuitable because of its high levels of salt, though some coastal hydroponic installations have used it successfully by thoroughly washing and leaching it first. If you wish to do this in a home garden situation you will need to chemically test the sand after washing and before use.

Sand used in hydroponic systems should not be excessively fine, since this can cause poor aeration and puddling, indicated by water coming to the surface upon vibration of the sand. The ideal sand aggregate is river sand, washed free of fine silt and clay. The particle size should be between 0.6 mm and 2 mm in diameter, which allows the aggregate to drain freely and not to puddle after an application of water. Some growers use a combination of sand sizes: 30 to 40 per cent of 5 mm, 40 to 60 per cent of 2 to 5 mm, and 5 to 15 per cent of 2 mm. Coarser sands offer faster drainage in cold, damp climates but can dry out rapidly in hot areas. Before using sand, wash it to remove any chemical impurities, dust and silt.

A hydroponic sand bed growing mustard lettuce.

ABOVE: A tropical garden highlighted by *Hippeastrum*. This hydroponic indoor garden uses small river pebbles and a simple micro-irrigation system to supply nutrients to plants. The trickle-irrigation aggregate system is easy to establish and maintain, and creates a natural and aesthetic garden.

BELOW: This crop of silverbeet is grown in a trickle-feeding system over a shallow bed of fine gravel. The system uses 19-mm poly pipe below and 2-mm spaghetti tubing to provide nutrients to the gravel bed. The pressure is controlled by a 19-mm shut-off valve positioned between the nutrient reservoir and main feed line. This system is easy to make and maintain.

This recirculating drip-irrigation system uses a mixture of aggregate (40 per cent nursery sand and 60 per cent blue metal). The system is fed from a central nutrient reservoir and 19-mm poly micro-irrigation pipe installed across the containers. The main irrigation line is fitted with adjustable drippers. The growing containers have been constructed using 25-litre plastic cubes cut in half. The watering cycle is fifteen minutes every two hours.

The simple Plant-A-Box system uses gravity to provide a regular flow of nutrients to these cherry tomato plants. The system uses no electrical or mechanical devices. The water is controlled by a 25-litre nutrient container which is sealed to provide a vacuum. Both the water inlet and air hose are positioned at the same level, about 2 centimetres from the bottom of the growing tray. Plants feed from the shallow pool of nutrients in the growing tray, and when the water level drops the air hose is opened, which in turn releases the vacuum in the nutrient container to allow more nutrients to flow into the growing tray. This system can be expanded by adding extra trays, connected by a water inlet hose only.

Sand-culture trials were being conducted as long ago as the mid-nineteenth century, and the first published attempt to develop the commercial potential of hydroponics, which occurred in America in 1929, used sand as the medium. Still widely used today, sand culture is well adapted to desert areas such as the Middle East and North Africa. Because of its low cost and its accessibility, it is widely used by home gardeners.

The sand culture system has many advantages. The fact that it is an 'open' (run-to-waste) system, whereby the nutrient solution is not recycled, greatly reduces the likelihood of diseases such as *Fusarium* and *Verticillium* spreading in the medium. It also prevents nutrient imbalance, as plants are fed with fresh nutrient solution at each irrigation cycle.

The excellent capillary action of sand results in lateral movement of the feeding solution so that there is an even distribution of nutrients throughout the root zone. Additionally, the smallness of the sand particles enables good water retention, necessitating fewer irrigation cycles during the course of a day. Practical advantages of sand culture include lower construction costs, simplicity of operation, and easy maintenance and service.

One of the few disadvantages of sand culture is the need to use chemical or steam sterilisation between crops in order to destroy medium-borne pathogens. Although time consuming, this method is at least thorough. Salt build-up is another common problem, but this can be corrected by flushing the medium periodically and carefully monitoring the drainage water for evidence of salt accumulation. For many home gardeners the greatest disadvantage of sand culture is the seemingly high consumption of nutrients because of the need to run to waste. However, with careful management, the waste should account for no more than 8 to 10 per cent of the total nutrient solution added.

A drip-irrigation system must be used with sand culture. Sand beds require a slight gradient (1:400), and a single 13-mm black polyethylene pipe is run down the length of the bed with micro 'spaghetti' lines inserted every 30 mm. In large beds, run the 13-mm poly pipe along the inside of each plant row.

Emitters can be used to deliver nutrients to plants, adjusted to deliver 4–6 litres per hour. A timer is required to deliver nutrients at regular intervals, which should be two to five times daily, depending upon the maturity of plants, weather and seasonal factors. Twice a week you should take a sample of the excess or drain-off and test it for total dissolved salts. If the

Puddling
Waterlogging, usually caused by fine sand. Puddling holds plant roots constantly immersed in nutrient solution, which can kill the plant.

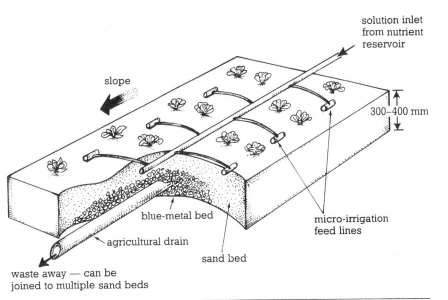

A cross-section of a sand bed.

dissolved salts reach 2000 parts per million, then you should use fresh water to leach the entire sand bed free of salts.

Sand beds can be constructed on any surface, including hard bedrock or stony ground. The beds should be lined with plastic, with a length of agpipe running down the centre to facilitate the removal of excess nutrients and water. Beds should be about 400 mm deep, with the agpipe buried in blue metal to prevent clogging. The nutrient tank should be large enough to meet feeding requirements for at least a week.

Sand culture is an ideal technique for Australian conditions, and is particularly well suited to rain-shadow areas. Sand beds tend to become water-logged during heavy rain periods in systems exposed to frequent rain, and should be sheltered using clear plastic film such as Solarweave or Solargro, or shadecloth.

Gravel

The characteristics of gravel are similar to those of sand, but the particles are larger. For this reason it does not hold water as well; but, as a corollary, it has much freer drainage. A combination of sand and gravel offers an excellent growing medium: ideally, 40 per cent sand to 60 per cent medium-sized blue metal, coarse river gravel or washed scoria.

Gravel culture is among the oldest and most widely used hydroponic techniques. It was one of the first methods used by W. F. Gericke, who pioneered the modern revival of soilless culture using sub-irrigation techniques. It was also the method used by the American GIs on non-arable islands in the South Pacific during the Second World War.

Gravel culture is often preferred to water culture as the aggregate helps to support plant roots. The aggregate is held in the same type of channel, tray or container as is used for water culture. The nutrient solution is held in a separate tank and pumped into the aggregate to moisten the roots as needed. After the aggregate has been irrigated, enough water and nutrients cling to the aggregate and roots to supply the plant until the next irrigation cycle.

As with sands, gravels of calcareous origin, such as limestone and coral, should be avoided, since they increase the alkalinity of the nutrient solution. This makes iron unavailable to the plants and also causes soluble phosphates in the solution to become insoluble.

The best choice of gravel is crushed granite of irregular shape or blue metal, free of fine particles less than 2 mm in diameter and coarse particles more than 15 mm in diameter. At least half the total volume of gravel should be about 10 mm in diameter. The gravel must be hard enough to resist breaking down over time, it must be able to retain moisture in the void spaces, and it must drain well to allow for good root aeration. Other types of gravel mediums include vermiculite, perlite, expanded clay, versarock, zeolite, pumice, smooth river-bottom pebbles, scoria, and crushed marble.

Gravel culture systems can be adapted to either NFT, using channel filled with gravel, and recycled nutrient solution; flood-and-drain or sub-irrigation systems; or drip-irrigation systems. (See Choosing a system.)

Vermiculite

The structure of vermiculite is similar to that of mica. This flaky mineral is mined in Africa, the USA and Australia. Flakes of raw vermiculite contain silicates of aluminium and iron. These flakes are heated in a furnace to very high temperatures in a process known as exfoliation. The moisture inside turns to steam, splitting the layers apart and creating light, spongy particles which are excellent for hydroponic cultures. The process expands the ore

gravel
bed

trickle-feed
system

submersible pump

Aggregate culture using gravel in a recirculatory or closed system.

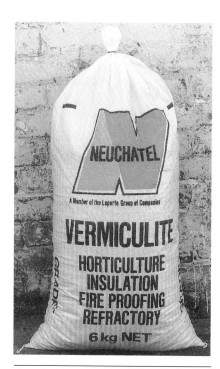

Vermiculite is available from nurseries and hydroponic stores.

particles some twenty-fold, and the very light, soft, glittering particles so formed will retain water up to 50 per cent by volume.

Vermiculite has a pH of 7.0, but it can at times turn slightly more alkaline. Like perlite, it is sterile and free from harmful organisms. Its excellent water retention properties make it an ideal additive to hydroponic mediums in situations where drying out is likely to be a problem. However, it should never be mixed wet because a deterioration in structure can result.

Vermiculite contains some magnesium and potassium, which it releases to the plants growing in it. It also has a relatively high cation exchange capacity and good buffering properties (that is, it can resist changes in pH).

The disadvantage of vermiculite is that, unlike other hydroponic mediums, it tends to break down over time, which might lead to clogging of tubing and filters in a recycling system, and drainage reduction leading to stagnation in simpler systems.

Perlite

Perlite is a volcanic mineral which resembles small, black crystals of sand when it is mined. On being heated to a temperature of 1000°C these crystals explode like popcorn and form soft white or grey granules which have a foam-like texture. The expanded material is very light, each particle being honeycombed with tiny air bubbles. These bubbles or air pockets can hold water or nutrients and then release them to the roots of plants. However, they are less spongy but better drained than vermiculite and the two mediums make a complementary mixture.

Among the more important features of perlite is sterility: when manufactured the material is free from disease and organic matter. Lightness is also a big advantage, making this material easy for the home gardener to handle.

The pH of perlite is fairly neutral — in the range of pH 6.5 to 7.5. Another vital feature is that it improves drainage of soils and provides the aeration that is so important to hydroponics. It can be used solely as a growing medium or, in situations where additional water retention is required, it can be used in conjunction with vermiculite, usually in a ratio of 2 to 1.

Unlike vermiculite, perlite has no cation exchange or pH buffering capacity and contains no mineral nutrients. It has a strong capillary attraction for water, making it an efficient user of sub-surface irrigation. The rigid structure of perlite gives it excellent aeration over its lifetime — which, with careful handling, can be many years.

Expanded clay

This medium is also known as LECA — light expanded clay aggregate. It is formed by blending and firing clay in rotary kilns and looks like small irregular balls. Expanded clay is a porous, lightweight substrate with excellent capillary properties. The internal structure quickly absorbs the nutrient solution, carrying it to plant roots, and the pebbles are light enough to ensure good air penetration, which prevents excess acidity and rotting. The structure and design of the pebbles also prevent decomposition and build-up of acids, and the pebbles have a very stable pH.

Expanded clay, because of its natural earthy appeal, is widely used as a growing medium for indoor potted plants and for many simple hydroponic systems. Where algae is a problem, however, the small pore size of expanded clay can cause clogging.

Although expanded clay is imported into Australia, its cost is not as prohibitive as it once was. As a result, it is proving a popular medium for more sophisticated systems, particularly for flood-and-drain tables, where it has proved an excellent medium.

Perlite is light and is often used with vermiculite as a growing medium.

Expanded clay is popular among home gardeners because of its excellent capillary properties and its natural look.

Aggregate culture

Aggregate mediums anchor plants and also retain solution between irrigations in different ways. Sand, perlite and vermiculite retain more solution than gravel, so irrigation frequency can be less with these substrates than with gravel. It should be noted that good aeration may be unsatisfactory if more than about 30 per cent of the particles are smaller than 0.5 mm.

Sands must be mainly quartz or other relatively inert materials. Calcareous sand that contains lime and/or dolomite is unsuitable unless it is thoroughly leached before use, and even then the pH of the solution may need frequent adjustment.

Versarock

This is a relatively new hydroponic medium which is derived from a volcanic ash of rhyolitic (granitic) composition. Mineralogically, it consists of kaolinite and opal C-T, with some other minor constituents. Essentially, Versarock is a naturally occurring 'premixed' ceramic.

Versarock is inert, is highly absorbent and can be milled to any particle size. It has an extremely porous structure but does not disaggregate in water. Air penetration through the medium is good due to the odd shape of the stones, which can have four, five or six faces, meaning that they do not 'marry' well. It is lightweight and has some cation exchange capacity.

One of the useful characteristics of Versarock is that it changes colour when dry, enabling the gardener to assess the moisture status of the system just by looking. The material has good insulating properties and is very slow to heat up and cool down, due to air entrapment within the pores. Versarock is inert and is easily pH stabilised. It is sterilised before sale and is user-friendly — it can be recycled again and again, and does not float or blow away in the wind.

Zeolite

Zeolite is a naturally occurring mineral which, because of its high cation exchange capacity, is used as a soil additive. Its use in hydroponics is not very wide yet, but it shows good potential as a medium.

The major minerals in zeolite are naturally occurring silicates. The material has an unusual 'cage-like' molecular structure and the ability to exchange plant nutrients freely. It is gravel like in appearance and reasonably heavy. Some research has been conducted in America into using a mixture of zeolite and another mineral, apatite, as a hydroponic medium.

Pumice

Pumice, like perlite, is a silicaceous rock of volcanic origin. It does not undergo any heating process. It is simply crushed and screened before use. Pumice is heavier than Perlite and does not absorb water as easily. It is sometimes used in a mix with peat and sand, but is a very good hydroponic medium on its own.

Expanded plastics

These materials are chemically inert and extremely lightweight. While several different types of plastic materials are used, generally they do not retain moisture or nutrient very well and, on their own, do not always provide sufficient support for plants. They can be mixed with other mediums, though some have a tendency to float to the top over time. Expanded plastics contain no nutrients, and have negligible cation exchange capacity and poor buffering capacity. Expanded plastics, sometimes called 'synthetic foams', are usually made from polyurethane, polystyrene or urea-formaldehyde.

While these are the main hydroponic substrates, others are used both in Australia and elsewhere, and new types are trialled regularly. River pebbles have characteristics similar to those of gravel and are popular with lettuce growers in Australia. Scoria is another medium derived from volcanic rock, though it tends to be rather heavy and dirty and needs washing.

Rockwool culture

Rockwool was developed by the Danish in 1969 and is now the most popular medium in Scandinavia. Worldwide, rockwool is used in over eighty per cent of hydroponic systems and it is also widely used as a propagation medium.

Rockwool culture appeared in Australia in 1982; now some forty-six hectares of crops are under commercial production — mainly cucumbers, tomatoes, strawberries, carnations and roses.

Rockwool is an inert fibrous material made from a mixture of volcanic rock, limestone and coke which is melted at a temperature of 1500°C to 2000°C. The molten substance is extruded as fine threads and pressed into sheets and then cubes. Surface tension is reduced by adding a phenol resin during cooling. A different form of rockwool is used in the building industry as an insulation material; this is not suitable for horticulture.

Horticultural-grade rockwool is noted for its good air- and water-holding capacity, containing about 3 per cent solid and 97 per cent pore space. Root growth tends to follow the direction of the fibres, and the fibre can be aligned either vertically or horizontally to suit the growth required. For propagation, the fibres are orientated in a vertical direction to allow downward root development. The cubes can then be placed on a slab to allow horizontal root development.

Rockwool is not biodegradable and contains no soluble materials. Therefore, as required it does not contribute nutrient or foreign substances to the culture system during use. The cation exchange capacity is negligible, so applied nutrients are not absorbed, and nutrient availability is dictated by the nutrient solution applied.

Rockwool has no pH buffer capacity; that is, it has no effect on the pH of the nutrient solution, other than when it is wet for the first time. On its initial wetting the rockwool will raise the pH of the solution by about 1 pH unit, which can be compensated if required. For feeding thereafter, a run-to-waste or rockwool-specific nutrient formulation can be used at a feed pH of typically 5.2 to 6.2.

Many users of rockwool condition the substrate to moisten the slabs uniformly and, according to some rockwool practitioners, to adjust the pH before transplanting and thus allow standard nutrient formulations to be used. That the pH is stabilised in this way is questionable, and rockwool-specific nutrients are recommended in preference to standard nutrients.

Conditioning is achieved by soaking the slabs in a nutrient solution for 24 to 48 hours. To do this, lay the slabs in their final resting position with three drip lines positioned at the top of each slab at equal spacing. Do not slit the sides or ends of plastic-lined slabs until the rockwool has been completely soaked in the nutrient solution.

Horticultural rockwool is available in many shapes and forms, ranging from small propagation cubes to slabs up to 1500 by 300 by 100 mm. Larger cubes are usually wrapped in plastic to prevent evaporation and the spread of roots into adjacent slabs. Large cubes can be obtained with a depression in the top into which smaller propagation cubes can be inserted for transplanting purposes. Granulated rockwool is also available for pot culture, or for adding aeration to potting mediums, used at the rate of 33 per cent of the medium volume.

Rockwool is an excellent inert substrate for both run-to-waste and 'recirculatory' systems. In run-to-waste systems the chance of disease spread is greatly lessened by the medium. Rockwool is also lightweight and self-

Rockwool culture is rapidly gaining popularity among home gardeners. Seeds can be started from small cubes, then transferred to larger cubes before final placement.

Rockwool culture

In wrapped rockwool installations, the drainage holes must be cut between the drippers and at both sides of the rockwool block. Ensure that the cut outlets under rockwool slabs are remote from drippers, so that the whole slab can be used and excess salts leached out.

Rockwool cubes are placed on top of slabs in this recirculatory rockwool system.

contained, which allows plants to be grown at different densities in different stages: young plants can be grown to an advanced stage in a small area before being planted out into the main growing area, thus improving crop turnaround. Its light weight also makes it quick and inexpensive to set up. Its lightness and rigidity eliminate the need for back-breaking work in preparation and planting.

The disadvantages of rockwool are few. Although relatively inexpensive, its bulk can make transport costs to remote regions prohibitive. However, the fact that it can be used several times over compensates for this by reducing overall costs.

To prevent minor skin irritation the user should wear gloves and a long-sleeve shirt and should wet the rockwool before handling it.

As in the case of NFT, plants can be propagated at a high density in small rockwool cubes in a specially regulated environment. They can then be spaced out into a moderately high-density area of the garden by placing these cubes on top of rockwool slabs positioned on benches or trays. Slabs can also be placed on the ground by using thick plastic between the soil and slab.

Rockwool culture does not demand an even surface as NFT does, as slabs are wrapped in polyethylene plastic which prevents drainage to the lowest area along the bed. In tropical climates the plastic is usually omitted to allow for evaporative cooling of the root zone. However, plastic is still used between slabs, to prevent wicking of the nutrient solution, a lack of solution in high spots and excess solution in low spots, and spread of any disease that might occur.

Narrow slabs (150 mm wide) are placed end to end in a double row to form a bed for cucumbers, tomatoes and roses. For other fresh flowers, wider slabs (300 mm wide) are used to line a bench. In both cases, cubes are used for individual plants, which are then placed on top of the slabs.

Plastic-lined slabs should be cut near the bottom of the sides, halfway between plants, as well as the ends of the slab. This will force nutrient solution to move horizontally throughout the slab.

Irrigation of the slabs can be via drippers, or by NFT, usually about three times a day. Ultimately, the frequency of irrigation will depend upon plant mass and weather conditions. For drip irrigation, the nutrient solution is delivered through microtubes from a PVC plastic pipe (15–20 mm) running along the bed.

A 150-mm thick slab of rockwool can hold about half of its pore space in water. However, the distribution of solution is unequal, with the lower part holding nearly all of the water and the top less than ten per cent. For 75-mm thick slabs, the water-holding capacity is 77 per cent of its pore space, leaving 20 per cent of the pores open for aeration.

Rockwool is an excellent medium for run-to-waste systems. This irrigation practice lessens the chances of disease since the nutrients are not recirculated. Additionally, much of the expensive solution-handling equipment and the electrical energy required by NFT are eliminated.

Rockwool can be re-used several times before it needs to be discarded. The salt content can be lowered for the next crop by applying only water during the last days of the existing crop. The old crop is then removed by twisting the cubes off the slabs. Rockwool can be used for one year for cucumbers and two years for tomatoes. If rockwool is to be used beyond these periods, it should be pasteurised (steamed under a plastic cover for thirty minutes).

Sawdust culture

Sawdust culture is mainly used in Canada and South Africa, and has been tried with mixed success here in Australia. Because of its low cost and light weight it has proved popular with some home gardeners. The main advan-

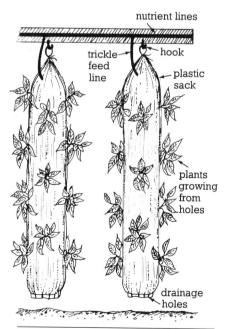

nutrient lines

trickle feed line

hook

plastic sack

plants growing from holes

drainage holes

A typical sawdust bag culture using trickle-irrigation methods.

tages of sawdust culture are the same as for sand culture: because it is an open system, there is less chance of disease, it has good lateral movement of the nutrient solution throughout the root zone, good aeration and high water retention.

Perfected by Canadian growers for tomato and cucumber production, sawdust culture is not without its problems, including pH imbalances. Additionally, over the cropping season salt may accumulate in the medium to toxic levels. This can be reduced by regular leaching with fresh water. Since sawdust is organic in nature, it also decomposes with time.

Not all sawdust can be used for hydroponic purposes; for example, Western Red Cedar (*Thuja plicata*) should be avoided because of potential toxicity. Moderately fine sawdust is best, typically from the Douglas Fir (*Pseudotsuga mensiesii*). Owing to microbial activity and chemical break-down, the sawdust needs to be replaced after each crop.

The two methods used for sawdust culture are the bed and bag system. The former uses moderately deep (200–250 mm) plastic trays with suitable drainage holes for run-to-waste feeding. Bag systems use polyethylene bags with holes punched in the bottom to allow good drainage. Depending upon the bag size, up to three plants can be grown in each bag. Bags can be either suspended from rafters, or set on the ground. A plastic sheet must separate the bag from the ground so that roots do not grow out the drainage holes and into the earth. Polyethylene garbage bags are frequently used by growers, but these must be set on the ground because of the weight of the sawdust. Twenty-litre plastic pots with drainage holes can also be used.

The ideal feeding system is drip irrigation or a trickle-feeding system. Seedlings can be started in rockwool cubes, then transplanted to the sawdust.

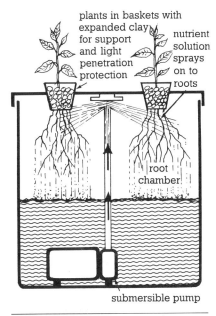

This is a schematic view of a conventional aeroponics system.

Aeroponics

The most recent development in hydroponics is aeroponics, defined by the ISOSC as a system in which the plants' 'roots are continuously or discontinu-ously in an environment saturated with fine drops (a mist or aerosol) of nutrient solution.' The method requires no substrate and entails growing plants with their roots suspended in a deep air or growth chamber, with the roots periodically wetted with a fine mist of atomised nutrients.

Since its development some thirty years ago, the aeroponic technique has proved very successful for propagation, but has yet to prove itself on a larger scale. It is widely used in laboratory studies of plant physiology, and is also being used in the USA to research controlled environment life support systems to be used in space stations of the future, and to support visitors to Mars.

The main advantage of aeroponics is the excellent aeration it gives. Trials of this system have detected a significant relationship between low water level and increased air space; the importance of oxygen in supporting the intensive metabolic processes associated with root formation and subsequent growth is well recognised.

Aeroponic techniques are noted for the development of large root structures.

Choosing a system

Roof-top gardening using an NFT system.

With the exception of the NFT system (see below) all hydroponic systems are suited to all plants. The choice depends on many factors — the size of your garden, the type of construction you prefer, how much automation you decide to use, and, of course, your budget. For example, for a small court-yard or balcony, where space is extremely limited, a system that is tiered will maximise the available space, allowing you to grow an array of plants to produce crops and/or enhance the aesthetics of the area. Construction type is a matter of cost and aesthetics; and the level of automation you choose is governed by your budget, and/or your commitment to maintaining such a garden on a regular basis.

Systems are categorised as either 'open' or 'closed'. An open (non-recirculatory) system is 'run-to-waste', which means that the nutrient solution passes the root zone only once before it is discarded. The most popular run-to-waste systems use gravel, sand, rockwool or sawdust as the medium. In closed systems the nutrient solution is continuously recirculated and can be adapted to NFT or rockwool systems, flood-and-drain tables, drip-irrigation systems or aeroponic chambers.

NFT system

The NFT system is a closed system and is simple to set up on a small scale. A large amount of water is required per plant and the solution must be aerated continuously. Various techniques can be used to aerate the nutrient solution, but it is usual to replace the solution at regular intervals or to agitate the solution with a small aquarium pump and air stone.

While the size, design and construction can vary between large commercial units, research laboratory units and units designed for the small home gardener, the basic principles of NFT remain the same. The essential components consist of a cultural vessel to hold the plant's roots, a nutrient reservoir, a submersible pump and irrigation fittings.

The most popular form of NFT system for the home gardener and commercial grower consists of rectangular, pre-fabricated rigid channels with removable lids. These channels can be set on simple, waist-high tables to allow easy access for the gardener. Rainwater downpipes also make practical channels, but they are difficult to clean between crops. Round PVC pipe and trays with curved bottoms have also been used; but, because of their shape, a nutrient film cannot be established and roots quickly block the flow of nutrient, leading to early flooding and waterlogging. Such channel profiles are not recommended, even though their low cost is tempting.

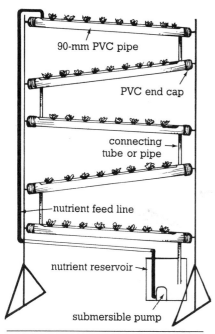

90-mm PVC pipe

PVC end cap

connecting tube or pipe

nutrient feed line

nutrient reservoir

submersible pump

Tiered NFT system, called a 'cascade'.

A variation of rigid channels is inexpensive black-and-white flexible plastic. The floor or surface needs to have a slight angle to permit the film of water to gravitate downwards to a collection receptacle from where it is recycled. Such channels need to be about 200 mm wide, with the two equal sides folded and supported across the top to form an inverted 'T'. The nutrient film flows along the floor of the channel. The black inside excludes light and the white exterior reflects light and heat. To assist crop establishment, a small piece of rockwool or capillary matting can be placed under young seedlings while roots develop.

A support wire, about 200 mm above the channel base, serves to keep the channel in shape and bolster young plants. During operation, the 'tent' shape must be maintained to allow adequate aeration. The plastic should not be allowed to collapse and make contact with the tops of the plant roots, otherwise air will be excluded from the channel.

Here are some of the different rigid channel profiles available to the home gardener.

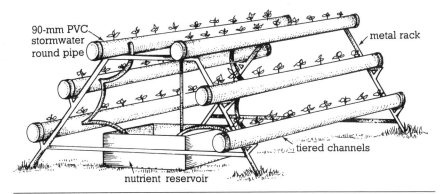

A-frame NFT system

Flood-and-drain system

The flood-and-drain (also known as sub-irrigation) system is a closed-system widely used by home gardeners, being especially suited to growing **herbs and seedlings**. The technique uses any of a variety of different media, including expanded clay, scoria, river pebbles, rockwool or pumice. It consists of a shallow table with an inlet and an outlet valve situated at the bottom of the tray. Once hourly, or less often according to the climatic and environmental conditions, the table is flooded for about fifteen minutes then drained to allow plant roots to aerate. Once the water level has reached a set depth during the flood cycle, an overflow valve allows the nutrient solution to drain back into a reservoir where it is recirculated by a pump, thereby providing a continuous flow of fresh nutrient solution to the plant roots.

The ebb-and-flow cycle of the nutrient solution pushes stale air upwards during the flood cycle, and pulls fresh air downwards to the root zone during the drain cycle. This movement of air and nutrient solution provides essential water, oxygen and nutrients to plant roots.

Unlike NFT, flood-and-drain systems have a greater buffering capacity in the event of breakdowns; that is, the medium holds a degree of moisture from which plants continue to derive nutrients until any malfunction is corrected.

The ideal frequency and duration of the flood-and-drain cycle is important to the success of the system and depends upon:
- the type of substrate
- the size of particles if using gravel
- the nature of the crop

A typical flood-and-drain or sub-irrigation system used for seedlings. Polystyrene is used here to float seedlings on the nutrient solution between watering cycles.

Drip- or trickle-irrigation systems

In drip- or trickle-irrigation systems, water is applied slowly and frequently to a limited part of the plant's root zone through devices such as drippers or emitters. The aim is to ensure that plants are never short of water and nutrients, so that they are able to grow as rapidly as other factors allow.

Advantages

- It is cheaper than other types of irrigation systems.
- Plant growth rates are high because plants need never be short of water and nutrients.
- If properly operated, less water and nutrients are used.
- Wind does not alter the distribution of water and nutrients.
- Work can continue in the area during irrigation cycles.

Disadvantages

- Drippers can clog.
- A filter must be used to remove particles from the nutrient solution.

This drip-irrigation system has an overhead main feedline, and 4-mm adaptor to provide irrigation to the medium and plant.

- the size of the crop
- environmental factors
- the time of day.

Large, coarse or smooth aggregate must be irrigated more frequently than porous, finely-shaped aggregate. Tall crops bearing fruit require more frequent flooding than short, leafy crops such as lettuce. Hot, dry weather and strong light promote rapid evaporation, calling for frequent irrigation. As a general rule, three to four daily irrigation cycles are adequate during winter, and as much as one irrigation cycle hourly is needed during the hot summer months. A couple of irrigation cycles are recommended during the night. Each cycle should last 10 to 15 minutes. Irrigation cycles should fill and drain the table rapidly, and drainage must be complete, with no residue solution left on the bottom of the bed or table.

The speed of flooding and draining of the nutrient solution determines the aeration of the plant root system. To respire the roots require oxygen, which in turn provides the energy plants need to take in water and nutrients. Insufficient oxygen around the roots can retard plant growth or cause plant injury, reduce yields, and even cause plant death. Essentially, the greater the movement of the nutrient solution, the greater the movement of air displacement.

Drip-irrigation system

Drip-irrigation (also called trickle-irrigation) systems can be open or closed, but most home gardeners prefer the open option. These systems can be easily designed and constructed with components readily available from the local hardware store. However, the nutrient must be entirely soluble in water, otherwise the micro-irrigation tubes and emitters might clog. Such systems can be used with a variety of substrates, including rockwool, expanded clay, gravel, sand, perlite/vermiculite, scoria, pumice, versarock, sawdust and zeolite. The watering regime is dependent upon the characteristic of the substrate as well as environmental factors.

The advantages of drip-irrigation systems include increased nutrient efficiency, low construction costs, reduced labour and energy costs, and greater flexibility in tailoring the timing of nutrient applications to crop demands, regardless of plant growth stages. Other advantages include good aeration in the root zone, since water trickling down carries fresh air with it and at no time are the roots submerged in water.

The main disadvantage of drip-irrigation methods is that some nutrients can cause clogging. A liquid concentrate is more suitable than powdered nutrients, but you should ensure that no sediment is resting at the bottom of the concentrate and that micro-nutrients are in chelated form to reduce the possibility of clogging. The use of an in-line filter in the main feed line will help reduce clogging.

If gravel is the main substrate, then 'coning' of water movement might sometimes occur due to the relative coarseness of the medium. This means that water flows straight down rather than moving laterally in the root zone. The result is a water shortage to plants and roots growing along the bottom of the bed where most water is present, eventually plugging drainage holes and pipes.

The bed design and construction of a drip-irrigation system are similar to those of sub-irrigation systems but simpler. The simplest system entails a 13-mm or 19-mm black poly tube running from the nutrient reservoir along the bed, which is then 'blanked' at the end of the garden bed. From this central irrigation line, 4-mm micro tubing (spaghetti tubing) is inserted at regular intervals. These irrigation lines must be long enough to reach the base of the plants that they are to feed.

To control the flow of the nutrient feed cycle, adjustable emitters can be used in the spaghetti lines or, alternatively, a tee and a tap can be inserted in the main irrigation line before it leaves the nutrient reservoir. The pressure flow of the system can then be controlled by opening or closing the tap. The advantage of the latter method is that excess water is returned to the reservoir, which in turn aerates the nutrient solution. Beds should be well drained, with excess nutrient solution either run to waste or returned to the nutrient reservoir for recycling.

Aeroponic system

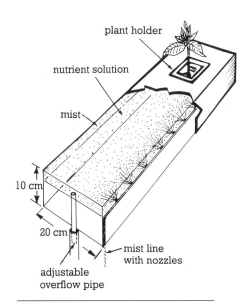

In aeroponics, plant roots grow in a closed chamber. A misting system bathes the roots in a film of nutrient solution and keeps them close to 100 per cent relative humidity to prevent drying. The chamber can be of any size and design, as long as it is moisture proof and dark. Tomatoes can be grown in tall, narrow containers lined with plastic. Lettuce and strawberries can be cultivated in A-frame containers to make the best use of space and light.

Apart from the relatively high set-up costs, the aeroponic technique is mechanically quite elaborate, susceptible to malfunction, requires regulation and control of water and nutrients, and has no buffer capacity to sustain even slight deviations or occasional malfunctions. If blocked nozzles or breakdowns go unnoticed, plants can be irreparably damaged in a relatively short time.

A schematic view of the Ein Gedi aeroponic system.

Yet, for propagation purposes, aeroponics is well proven. Experiments in Israel to assess aeroponics as a plant propagation method, and to determine the effect of dissolved oxygen on the rooting of cuttings, produced some interesting results. Both *Chrysanthemum* and *Ficus*, noted as difficult-to-root species, responded to increased dissolved oxygen concentrations. The number of roots and total root length increased as dissolved oxygen increased.

The Ein Gedi System (EGS), developed by workers of the Agricultural Research Organisation in Israel, is a trough system which utilises the advantages of true water culture systems to overcome the limitations of aeroponics and NFT, in effect combining the good points of all these systems.

The EGS is an aero-hydroponic, rather than a truly aeroponic, system, in which plant roots are immersed in a deep, circulating, continuously aerated nutrient solution. The solution is delivered in two layers: as a spray circulated on top of a liquid. The solution is injected into the trough by successive laser-cut apertures in a direction opposing that of the solution flow. Oxygen is carried from the spray zone into the nutrient solution, aerating it and providing high oxygen concentrations at the root surface. This permits roots to be immersed in a deep, large volume of nutrient solution, in troughs or channels of any length, and to grow in the spray zone.

The spray is created by injecting nutrient solution at relatively low water pressure through strategically placed nozzles. Aeration and delivery of spray vary according to the design of individual systems.

Commercial EGS installations are in operation in many countries, with tomatoes and cucumbers the major crops grown. The EGS system is also available as a propagation, hobby or laboratory unit and consists of an eighteen-litre cylindrical chamber (half-filled with continuously agitated water), motor and housing, and a removable cover with collared holes to support plants. It functions by drawing water up from the bottom centre of the container through a hollow, rotating impeller, driven by an electric motor. The rate of water uptake (two litres per minute) is proportional to the rotat-

The deep AeroFlo aero-hydroponic system in production with a capsicum crop.

The Rainforest modular aero-hydroponic system uses a circle of water to deliver nutrients to the root zone.

ing speed of the motor (300 rpm). The drawn water is then thrown horizontally by centrifugal force into the air space above the water reservoir, creating a fine spray and so increasing the water surface area. Then, as the water droplets fall back into the agitated water, gas exchange takes place.

Other types of aeroponic systems on the market include the Rainforest system, which is similar to the EGS system in its technology. It differs only in the mist or spray delivery. In this system a submersible pump draws water up a central tube to the top of the root chamber where the jet of water strikes a curved plate, causing the solution to be sprayed horizontally onto the roots in the spray zone. The circle (not a true spray) of water created then falls back into the reservoir to provide gas exchange.

Work in Australia and the USA has recently led to the development of an aeroponic system which uses ultrasonic technology to vaporise the nutrient solution, providing a fog-like mist to plant roots. The mist is much finer than any that can be achieved in conventional spray and pump systems. The main advantage of this system is that micro-irrigation equipment, which is prone to blockages, is eliminated.

Theoretically, aeroponics is a good system. However, the use of hydroponics overall is dictated by economic considerations and it is here that conventional aeroponics is cost prohibitive for most growing applications. The need for expensive timing, irrigation and pumping equipment puts it out of the reach of most home growers. For propagation and laboratory experiments, however, it is well proven and widely used.

Other systems

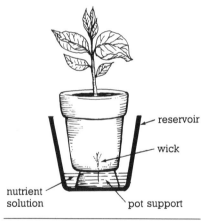

Wick system

Wick system

The wick system falls into the category of a closed system, and it is one of the most popular hydroponic options used by home growers. It consists of a double pot or container, with one section for the medium and the plant and the other for the nutrient solution. A fibrous wick, such as hemp rope or linen, is set into the growing container about one-third of the way, with the other end suspended in the nutrient solution below. As water evaporates from the foliage and moisture moves from the medium to the plant, capillary action draws more solution from the reservoir through the wick to the plant root zone.

Such a system can be easily designed for a balcony, a window ledge, or an under-used area of the garden, and supplied from a central nutrient reservoir. Though not essential, it is useful to have a floating marker to indicate the level of liquid in the reservoir.

Gravity/vacuum system

In recent years, the gravity/vacuum system has made its appearance, utilising an age-old principle of irrigation. It, too, is a closed system and consists of a growing tray and air-tight nutrient drum. The water inlet to the growing tray is level with an air hose which leads back to the nutrient drum. Gravity forces water into the growing tray to form a shallow pool of nutrient solution at the bottom of the bed. Once the nutrient pool reaches the level of the air hose, a vacuum is created in the drum, which in turn prevents any more solution from entering the growing bed. Then, as plants draw in nutrients and water, and some is lost to evaporation, the nutrient pool drops and exposes the air hose, which in turn releases the vacuum to allow more nutrients and water to flow into the growing tray.

The gravity, or Vacuum Plant-a-Box system, uses no electrical or mechanical devices. These systems can be expanded using the same nutrient reservoir.

In order for the gravity/vacuum system to function correctly, both the growing bed and nutrient drum must be at the same level. Such systems are economical to construct or purchase and make an ideal entry point for beginners to learn the basic principles of hydroponic cultivation before moving on to more complex systems.

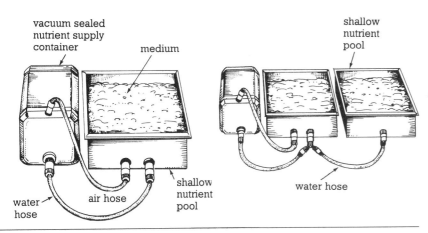

This is a typical design for a gravity/vacuum system. It is the basic principle used by farmers to maintain the water level in chicken sheds.

Gravity-feed system

The gravity-feed system, which can be open or (more popularly) closed, has proven popular with home gardeners owing to its low cost and simplicity of construction and operation. The key to its success is the nutrient reservoir, which is positioned higher than the growing tray, and a collection reservoir positioned lower than the growing table. The nutrient solution flows from the reservoir into the aggregate material in the growing bed, from where it drains into the collection receptacle. The nutrient solution is then returned to the nutrient reservoir using either a foot pump or an electrical submersible pump. The keen gardener can interchange the nutrient container and the collection container at regular intervals, eliminating the need for any electrical devices.

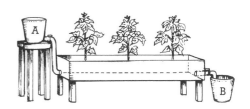

Simple gravity-feed system. The solution flows from A into the aggregate substrate in the growing table. When the growing table is flooded, the solution is drained into B, then returned to A, either manually or electrically.

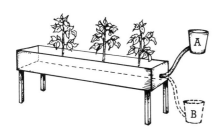

Manual gravity-feed system

Self-watering pots

Several examples of this closed system are available on the market, and are a good way of entering the world of hydroponics. The three most popular types of self-watering pots are the Decor range, in which a see-through, deep saucer is attached to the main pot, and the Luwasa and Leni hydroculture pots, which use a water gauge to indicate the level of the nutrient solution within the pot. These pots generally use expanded clay as the growing medium because of its aesthetic appeal and good capillary action.

The self-watering pot is the perfect system for indoor plants. The Leni and Luwasa pots consist of an inner and an outer pot, with the former perforated down the sides to allow the plant's roots to aerate and to feed from the nutrient solution. Once the plant has outgrown its pot, the inner pot can be easily removed and placed in a larger outer pot which is then filled with more expanded clay.

Building a system

The simplest and most inexpensive way to grow vegetables, herbs and flowers hydroponically is to use plastic or polystyrene trays. The latter can be easily obtained from fruit and vegie shops and adapted to become a series of hydroponic garden beds. The best kind are broccoli boxes because they have no drainage slits on the bottom. However, you will need to prepare such trays and boxes with drainage holes about two centimetres from the bottom to provide a shallow nutrient pool from which the plants can draw their nourishment. The concept is the same as for self-watering pots, or a standard terracotta pot and saucer.

You can hand-water the trays as required, or install a simple irrigation system to handle automatic irrigation. Simple micro-irrigation fittings are readily sold over the counter at nurseries and garden centres. The nutrient reservoir usually consists of a small plastic pail or drum, and a fish-aquarium submersible pump will distribute the nutrient solution to the garden beds.

To build a simple run-to-waste system, you can use polystyrene boxes with existing drainage slits. Simply fill the boxes with sand and install a trickle irrigation feeding system in the manner just described. Irrigation cycles should be timed so that excess nutrient accounts for no more than ten per cent of the total nutrient solution. You can measure this by placing a small cup or container beneath one box to capture excess nutrients. At the end of each watering cycle, the cup should not overfill with excess nutrients. This technique might take a few days of trial and error, but you can start with a watering regime of three minutes to every hour.

Once you are satisfied that hydroponics is for you, you can design more elaborate systems or upgrade and expand your current enterprise.

NFT system

A number of small NFT systems are already available on the market, and there are some compelling arguments in favour of purchasing these — most obviously the convenience of a complete kit that is ready to plug in. For the aged and infirm, or for anyone who leads a busy life, a ready-to-go NFT kit is a practical solution. However, you can also custom build your own NFT system according to your specific requirements.

The actual design of your NFT system is limited only by your imagination. But bear in mind that the system must provide a means to:
- support the plant above the solution
- deliver the nutrient solution
- aerate the nutrient solution
- prevent light from reaching the solution so that algae doesn't grow.

NFT system using 90 mm stormwater pipe.

Channel slope

The NFT channel slope must be firm and regular to avoid pools of nutrient solution forming. In such pools, plant roots lose contact with the atmosphere and show symptoms of waterlogging.

A minimum slope of 1:50 is widely accepted; however, a slightly higher slope is more desirable. In practice a higher slope may be more difficult to achieve due to the extra lift required by the pump. There is no maximum slope, and many successful crops have been grown in vertical NFT systems. The only major obstacle to such systems is the ability to hold firmly plants in the channel.

Channel width

For the healthy growth of tomato plants, narrow channels can be dismissed. In soil, you can see that tomato plants produce large root systems. In hydroponic systems it is no different. To grow tomatoes, the channel needs to be at least 20 cm wide at normal spacing to accommodate the abundant roots. Such widths can be constructed at ground level using thick black or white plastic to form the channels.

To construct your own NFT system you will need a certain level of skill, but for many people the task is easy and enjoyable. The size of the installation is important, with most home gardeners settling on a system somewhere between two and five metres long and three to five channels wide. Long runs of channel are not recommended, since they generate heat gradients in the channel, can slow down the speed of circulation, and do not adequately aerate plants at the end of the channel. The site of the system should also be protected from wind. If such a location is not possible, then a wind screen will prove beneficial.

If adopting a bench or table design, a good working height is sixty-five to seventy-five centimetres, which will enable you comfortably to reach from one side of the table to the other. Aesthetic appeal might also be an important consideration. Other designs include A-frame, tier or wall-tier. Each has its merits, and they are all popular with home growers.

If the site for the proposed system has awkward characteristics, such as a steep incline, soft soil or a dog-legged shape, these will need to be addressed — the ground will need to be filled, the bench footings will need to be anchored with cement to prevent the table from sinking and upsetting the flow of nutrients through the channel, and so on.

This typical small NFT system is easy to construct and operate.

Channel layout

The standard form of NFT system uses rigid channels, but simpler systems can be constructed using standard trays. For multiple-row channels, the separation should be between ten and thirty centimetres, depending upon the plant being cultivated. The size of the channel is also important. Configurations vary from 50 mm wide and 40 mm high to 150 mm wide and 70 mm high. Wider channels, resembling rainwater downpipe, can also be purchased. The size of the channel that is used will govern the type of plant that can be cultivated. For most standard-size channels, plants that can be grown successfully include lettuce, endive, strawberries and parsley. Plants such as tomatoes and cucumbers are less successful owing to their large root structures, which can cause channel blockage and 'pooling'.

Channels or trays should have a slope of 1:30 to 1:50 to prevent ponding and waterlogging, although this might still occur as plant roots mature. The slope can be provided by the floor, benches or racks.

...arsley grown in a hanging 'Green Genii'. ...his closed system is constructed from ...astic and filled with perlite. The growing ...ints in the tube are specially designed to ...low nutrients to flow down the centre of ...e tube, and not to spill out of the growing ...ints. Nutrients are fed to the plants via ...removable cup with fine holes in the ...ottom, which is located inside the top of ...e Green Genii. The solution trickles ...rough the cup, down the tube, and ...llects in a removable cup at the bottom ...the system. Once daily, the bottom cup ...removed and the solution recirculated.

...typical flood-and-drain table is used here ...trial different mediums for growing ...nnamon basil. The different mediums ...clude versarock (bottom far left), ...xpanded clay pebbles (bottom left), zeolite ...ottom centre) and pumice (bottom far ...ght).

Limonium 'Misty Blue' is often used as a filler flower in floral arrangements. Easy to grow, and with a tolerance to varied conditions, this crop is being grown in recycled rockwool, which is simply placed in a black plastic bag on the ground. This simple system uses a run-to-waste drip-irrigation system, the wastage reduced to 10 per cent of the total solution.

Marigold is an ideal companion plant to deter whitefly infestations. These flowers are grown in a simple hand-watering system using a mixture of perlite and vermiculite. The growing tray has two small overflow holes at each end, about 2 centimetres from the bottom to allow the medium to drain quickly during periods of rain.

ABOVE: Strawberries growing in a home-made NFT system constructed of PVC stormwater down-guttering. The strawberries were propagated in 75 × 75 mm rockwool cubes, which were then transplanted to the NFT system. The top of the guttering has been cut away at regular intervals to facilitate the rockwool cubes. The cubes are covered with reflective tape to prevent light getting into the channel and, therefore, stopping the growth of algae.

ABOVE: Brussels sprouts growing in a recirculating aggregate system. The main substrate is blue metal which provides good drainage and aeration. Brussels sprouts are a heavy feeder, requiring a conductivity between 1750 and 2100 parts per million (cF 25–30). These plants are fed via a trickle-irrigation system.

LEFT: Chinese turnips as large as apples growing in a combined sand and blue metal aggregate. The method of irrigation is drip using 13-mm black micro-irrigation tubing. The watering regime is fifteen minutes at two hourly intervals. The system is set at waist height for easy access.

BELOW: Coral lettuce is a popular, quick-growing lettuce. This crop is growing in an NFT system using four different types of channel profiles to determine growth rates. All lettuce varieties are low feeders, with best results achieved at around 700 parts per million (cF 10) nutrient strength.

ABOVE: There are a variety of home hydroponic units available to hydroponic enthusiasts. These can be purchased from specialist hydroponic stores, or easily constructed from bits and pieces often found around the home.

BELOW: This hobby gardener has taken advantage of his environment to construct an apparatus to support his tomato plants. Other types of plant supports include reinforced concrete wire or large gauge chicken wire or netting. For ground-level hydroponic systems, a trellis can be easily constructed using a series of tight wires along the length of the growing bed, strung between two fence posts.

As a general rule, flow rates for each channel should be around one litre per minute. The rate might vary from installation to installation, but it should be at least half a litre per minute and no more than two litres per minute. Flow rates outside these parameters can cause nutritional problems.

There is no strict watering regime, and irrigation cycles vary from one grower to another. While most NFT systems use a continuous watering cycle, some growers prefer intermittent cycles, with a few minutes of irrigation every ten to twenty minutes. Intermittent cycles increase aeration in the root zone, but on hot days there is a fine line between good aeration and dry roots.

Reservoir volume

The ideal volume of working nutrient solution in the reservoir depends on the type of plant being cultivated and is critical to the smooth and effective running of NFT. As a general rule, allow around one litre of nutrient solution per plant; for example, if you are growing twenty plants, then the nutrient solution volume should be at least twenty litres. Less might cause plants to take up substantially more water than nutrients, and more might do the opposite, increasing or decreasing nutrient concentration over a short period of time. An increase in nutrient concentration can cause root injury, while a decrease will slow down the growth of the plants. Also, major changes in nutrient concentration are linked to substantial pH changes, which can shock the plants.

Reservoir site

The nutrient reservoir determines the direction of flow in the channels. It must be the lowest component of any NFT system and must be covered so that rainwater does not dilute the nutrient solution.

Solution temperature

The ideal solution temperature varies from one plant to another. However, for most plants it should stay between 18°C and 25°C. There is a danger that the solution will overheat if the channel is exposed to too much direct sun during the hot summer months. As plants mature, they will shade the channel to some degree, making overheating less likely.

Flood-and-drain system

Flood-and-drain systems are easy to construct and operate, and may consist of flood-and-drain tables or trays, or a bucket arrangement. Both set-ups can be expanded as required, but they must be designed to provide rapid filling and draining. To achieve this, the water inlet and outlet lines should be at least 19 mm in diameter. A timer is needed to control the pump and the irrigation cycles. All storage tanks and delivery lines should be opaque to reduce algae growth.

Flood-and-drain tables

Flood-and-drain tables may consist of single or multiple trays positioned at the same level, or terraced trays with each successive level lower than the one before it. The latter method is ideal for uneven ground, or for gravity-feed systems. The bottom of a higher bed should be level with the top of the lower bed.

Building tips

- Building a hydroponic system, like any other activity, can be a lot easier and more enjoyable if you have the right tools and equipment.
- When selecting a hydroponic system, the main consideration should be maintenance time. A small recirculating system which can grow up to 50 plants requires about 10 minutes work per day; to check the pH and nutrient level, and to renew the nutrient solution from time to time.
- Only plant what you are likely to need during the harvest period. On deciding how much to plant, picture the harvest. If you can only use four cabbage and six lettuce during the four week harvest period, then plant only your requirement. If you are unsure of their possible success, add a few more for extra protection, but never more than twice as many as you want to harvest.

Environmental protection

Climate is one major variable you can't control: the plants do not get enough sun; frost wipes out your capsicums earlier than you expected; the weather turns cold in spring, and your tomatoes don't grow well for several weeks; or the wind destroys some of your plants.

In a hydroponic garden, you can modify or move your garden to improve the growing conditions. This may mean making a simple windscreen, adding a reflector to supply more light, heating the growing medium to speed up germination, or using a variety of devices to protect plants from frost and extend either end of the growing season.

Garden reflectors

Most vegetables need a minimum of 6–8 hours of direct sunlight a day to grow properly. Unfortunately, small city gardens may be jammed between a fence and a wall, sandwiched between two buildings, or crammed into an oddly-shaped corner so plants are shaded most of the day. If you have this problem, don't give up. You can add to the natural light with a reflector panel or wall.

Make reflector panels by stapling or gluing aluminium foil, or similar materials, to large sheets of cardboard or plywood. Make the reflector panel the same length as the hydroponic garden. If there is a wall, paint it white. Not only will it reflect light, but it will also provide a degree of heat which can be beneficial to the growing season.

Growing beds should have a minimum depth of 120 mm. The overflow valve should be set so that the table floods to within 10 mm of the top of the substrate before it overflows back to the nutrient reservoir in the case of a single tray, or into the next table in the case of terraced trays.

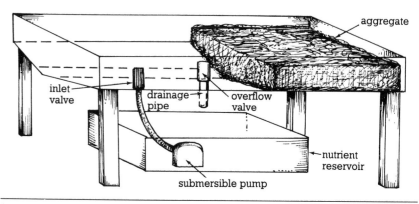

A simple flood-and-drain table which is fed from below by a submersible pump.

Nutrient reservoir

In the case of single or multiple trays at the same height, the nutrient reservoir is positioned underneath the first table, and uses a submersible pump to distribute the nutrient solution. For terraced tables or trays, the nutrient solution is stored in an above-ground header tank raised a metre or more above the level of the first tray or bed. An automatic solenoid or manual gate valve is used to control the flow of solution. The nutrient solution flows through the system and collects in a sump, from where it is pumped back into the raised header tank.

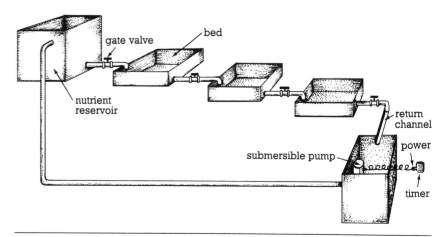

This is a terrace flood-and-drain-system. The nutrient solution is returned to the main nutrient reservoir once the system has drained.

Drip-irrigation system

You can construct a simple drip irrigation system using a growing tray, nutrient reservoir and trickle feeding system operated by a pump on a timer. A typical drip irrigation system uses gravel and/or sand, perlite/vermiculite, expanded clay or sawdust as a medium. Each of these substrates has its strong points, with the choice being governed by budget.

Beds

Beds can be constructed at ground level, or may be adapted using trays or even a child's swimming pool. A typical ground bed should have an approximate width of 1 metre and a depth of 400 mm. The slope of the bed should be about 1:400 to allow for good drainage of excess nutrient solution. The bed should be filled to within 20 mm of the top at the end near the nutrient tank and within 40 mm at the other end. If the bed is filled evenly, it will cause uneven watering of plant roots.

Ground beds can be constructed easily using wooden planks or concrete reinforcement wire, bent at the sides and ends to form the gravel bed itself. Each gravel bed should be lined with black plastic or swimming pool liner to prevent the nutrient solution from leaching into the bare ground. If you are using black polyethylene film, you should double it over for maximum strength — a single layer of film will stretch and tend to mould around sharp objects once gravel or sand is shovelled into the bed, which may cause it to rupture. A perforated, 90-mm drain pipe or 'agpipe' should be set the entire length of the bed, which in turn should be connected to a main pipe at one end to collect waste water and to conduct it away from the growing area. If you are using sand, you should cover the drain pipe with blue metal to prevent clogging and to help discourage plant roots from entering the pipe.

Nutrient reservoir

The nutrient reservoir should be watertight and hold a volume thirty to forty per cent more than the total volume required to fill the bed. You can attach an automatic float valve to the water refill line in order to top up the reservoir. Nutrient can be delivered either by gravity or by means of a submersible pump. Drain the reservoir periodically and remove any sludge or sediment that has accumulated owing to impurities in the nutrient salts.

Irrigation lines

For small garden beds, a single 13-mm black polyethylene pipe can be run down the length of the bed with spaghetti lines inserted every 300 mm. For gravel systems, each plant will require a single spaghetti line. Larger beds will require 13-mm poly pipe along the inside of each plant row, from which the spaghetti lines run.

Emitters can be used to deliver nutrients to plants, adjusted to deliver four to six litres per hour. Alternatively, spaghetti lines can be inserted into the main 13-mm feed line. For sand culture systems, a short length (50 mm) of 13-mm poly tube can be attached to the end of each spaghetti line to channel nutrients to each side of the irrigation point. Emitters, above ground pipes and fittings should be black to prevent algae growth inside the piping system. Algae will rob nutrients of oxygen and minerals in the presence of light.

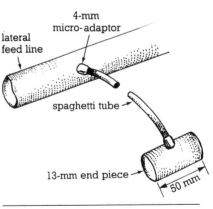

'Spaghetti' micro-irrigation line which is used for drip- or trickle-irrigation systems.

Irrigation cycle

The irrigation system should be capable of delivering six to ten litres of nutrient solution per minute. If you use a timer, you should programme it to deliver nutrients two to five times daily, depending upon the maturity of plants, weather and seasonal factors. Once a week a sample of the run-off should be taken and tested for total dissolved salts. If the dissolved salts reach two thousand parts per million, then the entire bed should be leached free of salts using fresh water or a mild solution of nutrients.

Rockwool layout

The layout for a recirculating rockwool system is fundamentally the same as for a run-to-waste rockwool system. It is necessary to collect what would otherwise be the drainage and to re-direct it back into the supply side of the irrigation system.

This can be achieved by setting slabs into a polyethylene-line gully on the ground or by raising the slabs onto channels or benches from which the run-off solution is collected. In either case, the slope of the run should be regulated to give a reasonable water-to-air ratio within the slabs.

Rockwool system

Rockwool systems can be either run to waste or recirculatory. Because of the high water-holding capacity of this substrate, you can get away with feeding it less frequently (once daily) than other mediums. However, it is better management to feed several times a day — the exact number depending on the crop under cultivation. Frequent irrigations are required just after transplanting. Then, once plants become established, five to ten times daily should suffice, increasing to twenty times daily in summer. Irrigation should continue until ten to twenty per cent of excess nutrient solution drains from the slab.

Run to waste

For run-to-waste rockwool systems, the best floor is of levelled concrete, with a slight slope on each side inclined towards the centre. This type of floor allows good drainage away from the slabs, good light reflection, and good hygiene. An adequate catchment area should be provided to channel excess nutrients away from the growing area. Soil or sand floors are also suitable but should be levelled in the same manner, thoroughly disinfected and covered with thick white plastic sheeting to give good light reflection as well as hygiene.

Rockwool beds should be spaced at one-metre intervals to allow good access between beds. The nutrient solution is delivered to the base of each plant with micro irrigation lines (2–4 mm), supplied from a rigid PVC pipe, or a 19-mm poly irrigation line running along each bed and fed from a central nutrient reservoir.

Recirculation

Rockwool recirculatory systems are rapidly gaining popularity among home growers. Using the same fundamental drip irrigation techniques as for rockwool run-to-waste systems, recirculatory systems vary only in their configuration. They range from slabs placed on trays with a 1:200 incline to allow the slabs to drain, to self-draining growth modules. In either situation the nutrient solution is captured and recirculated at regular intervals.

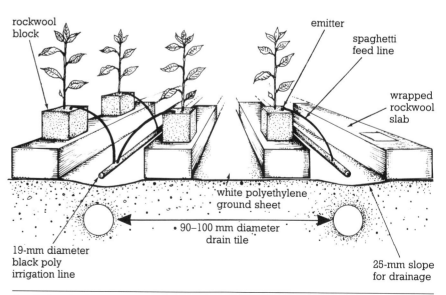

A typical recirculatory rockwool system.

Aeroponic system

Aeroponic systems can be easily constructed using 20-litre buckets or a deep tray; a submersible pump; an air pump and an air stone; and spray nozzles. The spray nozzles must be positioned within the chamber so that at least a portion of each plant's roots is sprayed directly. The nozzles may be left on at low pressure continuously or operated intermittently, on for one minute and off for two minutes.

An A-frame aeroponic system can be constructed and is illustrated on the left. This type of design makes the most of available space and light. Each side of the panel should have a series of 50-mm holes drilled to accommodate net-like pots with their seedlings. Additionally, the A-frame should be hinged so that each side of the panel can be raised to facilitate easy micro-irrigation and pump maintenance, and cleaning between crops.

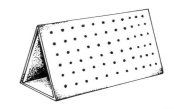

A-frame aeroponics system. Each panel is pre-drilled with 50-mm hole to fit small growing containers.

Electrical pumps

In hydroponics, pump choice is of fundamental importance and is directly related to the nature of your system, be it flood and drain, NFT, aeroponics or drip. Pumps are basically divided into two types — positive displacement and rotodynamic. Rotodynamic pumps are further divided into three categories: centrifugal, mixed flow and axial flow.

In hydroponic systems, the main types of pumps used are rotodynamic, and of these the centrifugal pump is the most common. This is the most efficient pump for pumping large volumes with relatively low lifts — precisely what is needed by most small-scale hydroponic systems. Centrifugal pumps do not actually encapsulate a volume of fluid in order to pump it, but rely on what is called 'hydrodynamic action'. The impeller is enclosed in a chamber called the volute, which has two openings: the inlet and the outlet (see diagram below). To this is connected the motor, which drives the axle that the impeller sits on. Spinning action produced by the impeller forces water through the outlet, then draws it back in through the inlet. The centrifugal pump is designed so that it can drain back through itself. These pumps by their nature are not self priming, so they should be either submerged or placed in line — preferably below the reservoir.

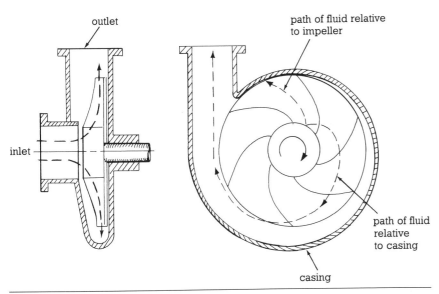

Cross-section of a typical centrifugal pump.

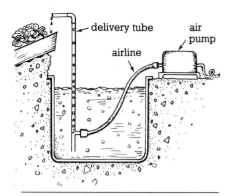

Simple layout for an airlift system.

Electrical safety

Electrical safety is extremely important in any powered hydroponic system since water and electricity are a lethal combination. Most systems require electricity on site to drive appliances such as pumps and heaters and, while systems do not require any special electrical installation, the reality is that the growing environment itself does not favour electrical safety and there is an increased risk of electrical shock from faulty supply or appliances. This is because the hydroponic environment tends to have high humidity, and floor surfaces might be damp. As such, an automatic earth leakage detector circuit breaker should be installed for use between the mains supply and the electrical equipment.

The choice most purchasers face is whether to use a submersible or an open-air pump. Submersible pumps are the most popular because they are easy to install, quiet to operate and very efficient, and they require very few fittings. The only disadvantage of the submersible pump is its proximity to water and nutrients. Because of this both the casing and the shaft must be sealed against the possible ingress of solution. While the casing is easy to seal, the shaft is more difficult. Also, nutrient salts are aggressive and can reduce seal life. Suitable pumps are constructed of ABS plastic and are fitted with chemically resistant seals and no metallic parts.

Open-air pumps generally need fittings that are more precise and more expensive. Most either need to be primed or require that the inlet to the pump head be flooded. While this is easy when the pump is running, starting the pump is in fact when the problem occurs. One way to overcome this is to install the pump well below the solution level in the reservoir. Larger non-submersible pumps are generally much easier to fit.

An alternative to both submersible and non-submersible pumps is an air-lift system which uses a simple and inexpensive air pump. Properly rigged, the air-lift system of pumping works by displacing water with air. The main disadvantage of the air-lift system is that the solution is not moved under pressure and so cannot easily be distributed to several channels or outlets. Accordingly, a separate

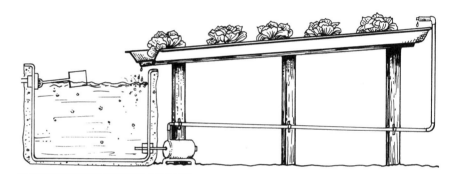

Layout for non-submersible pump, ensuring a flooded inlet.

air pump needs to be provided for each irrigation outlet. Although it can be costly and complex, this is ideal for systems that have a single irrigation point, such as a single-channel NFT system. While the air-lift system cannot be used for draining the reservoir, unless drainage by gravity can be arranged, and it is susceptible to a falling solution level in the reservoir, its overriding advantage is that it introduces aeration into the nutrient solution, thereby adding oxygen.

When designing a system, you should take care to ensure maximum efficiency, resulting in fewer problems and lower operating costs. This is achieved through uniformity of pipe diameter, and a minimum of bends and fittings.

Filters

Filters are an essential component in any drip irrigation system. In-line filters, such as those manufactured by Hardie Pope and Nylex, should contain at least a hundred mesh screens which can be removed and cleaned periodically. The filter should be installed in-line, soon after the submersible pump. Alternatively, or additionally, the pump can be placed in a filter bag, such as those available from selected hydroponic stores. A nylon stocking will also serve as a practical filter substitute.

Planting

Although large-scale commercial hydroponic systems might appear daunting to the novice, they are really quite simple in construction and operation. Small-scale systems designed along the same lines can be set up on a patio, on a rooftop, or in the backyard with very little effort. Plants grown in an outdoor system should be started during the season recommended for normal soil gardens. However, where the environment can be controlled, indoor crops can be grown year-round.

Hydroponic systems will not compensate for poor growing conditions such as inappropriate temperature, inadequate light or pest problems. Remember, hydroponically grown plants have the same general requirements as field-grown plants, the only major difference being the method by which the plants are supported and supplied with nutrient.

Seed germination

Large seeds can be planted directly into aggregate culture systems or do-it-yourself propagators. To ensure a good stand, small seeds should be sown in rockwool or a mixture of perlite and vermiculite first, then transplanted into the hydroponic system as seedlings. With water culture methods, plants must not be transplanted into the system until they have developed an adequate root structure.

Seeds can be sown in sand, vermiculite, perlite or rockwool. Water them and cover or seal them with either wet paper towels or Gladwrap until they germinate. Alternatively, you can invest in or manufacture your own mini-propagator. Once the seeds have germinated, remove the cover and thin them. Use a dilute nutrient solution rather than water to moisten the young seedlings as required because the germination medium is not designed to provide nutrition. When the seedlings are large enough to transplant, gently wash any growing medium other than rockwool from their roots, but do not be too concerned if fragments of the medium remain. Seedlings germinated in soil and purchased from your local nursery can also be transferred to hydroponics. Simply wash the soil from the roots, taking care not to damage the fine hairs.

Seedlings to be transferred into most systems can be grown with their roots exposed or in rockwool cubes. If you want to transfer them to water culture or aeroponic systems it is best to grow them with their roots protruding from the growing pot or rockwool cubes. Seedlings destined for water culture channel should be grown in rockwool cubes such as 'Growool' propagation starters or a compressed mixture of perlite and vermiculite. These

The EGS aeroponic system is ideal for propagation.

Seeds can be planted into rockwool propagation blocks which are then transplanted to the hydroponic system once the seeds have germinated.

Cuttings should be green barked and should not contain any of the woodier type bark which indicates age. They should be 10–15 cm tall with three to five sets of well-developed leaves and a sprout at the top.

substrates provide weight and help to support the plant in the channel. The substrate also blocks light from the roots, preventing damage and discouraging the formation of algae in the channel.

Cloning

The practice of cloning, whereby one cell of a plant is isolated by means of a cutting and grows into another plant, is recognised as one of the most efficient and productive methods of plant propagation in hydroponics. Whereas seeds are produced by sexual propagation, cloning results in asexual or vegetative propagation. The resultant plant is genetically identical to the host from which the cutting came, provided it is grown in exactly the same environment as the parent plant. Cuttings from the same plant grown in different growing environments will develop different characteristics.

Cuttings can be taken from any plant, regardless of age or growth stage. However, cuttings taken from young vegetative-stage plants root and grow quickly, whereas cuttings taken from a flowering plant usually root a little more slowly.

Cloning is achieved simply by taking a cutting from a plant, dipping it into a rooting compound to minimise antimicrobial activity, and placing it into a growing medium such as rockwool or a perlite/vermiculite mix. Cuttings can be taken from anywhere on the plant but stems should be no thinner than 4 mm and no thicker than 6 mm for best results. New cuttings should then be fed a half-strength nutrient solution.

Healthy cuttings will retain almost all their leaves; however, it is natural for some leaves to die off during the rooting process. The cuttings should develop a good root structure within two weeks. After the second week, cuttings should be fed full-strength nutrient.

Take care not to overwater or underwater new cuttings. Overwatering will cause roots to rot, and underwatering will cause them to shrivel. Healthy roots are thick, white and hairy looking. Damaged roots are thin, yellowish or brown, and have no root hairs. Once full strength nutrient is applied, it is a good idea to start balancing the nutrient solution to about pH 6.0 to 6.5.

Once plants have developed adequate roots, they should be transplanted to their hydroponic system and started on a regular feeding schedule. If using rockwool cubes, do not remove the rockwool, but transplant direct into the hydroponic system, whether NFT, rockwool, aggregate or aeroponic.

Seedling and cloning shells can be easily made from an old aquarium.

Transplanting from soil

Plants can be easily transplanted from soil mediums to a hydroponic system. Simply wash away excess soil in luke-warm water, taking care not to damage the fine hair roots of the plant. The success rate of transferring soil-grown plants to hydroponics might be lower for mature plants which have developed a large tap root, as this is easily damaged when the plant is removed from the soil.

In hydroponics, plants develop a capillary-like root structure rather than large tap roots. This is because nutrients are readily available and plants do not have to stretch out and search or compete for available nutrients as they do in soil. Therefore, the younger the plant, the more readily it will adapt to hydroponics. Plants with large, complex root structures will find it difficult to adapt to a hydroponic medium and will have a high mortality rate. It is far better to take a cutting from the plant for hydroponic cultivation.

Cloning material should have the lower leaves removed.

Nutrient solutions

Premixed nutrient solutions are available from a number of sources, including the local nursery and specialist hydroponic stores located throughout the major centres of Australia and New Zealand. They are relatively inexpensive and easy to use. As you become more familiar with growing plants hydroponically, you might wish to make your own nutrient solutions. Again, the raw elements are readily available from specialist hydroponic stores.

As plants take up nutrients, they release into the solution chemicals or by-products that might make it more alkaline. When the pH rises above 7.0, you should add small quantities of phosphoric acid or nitric acid to bring it back to a pH between 5.5 and 6.5. For large plants it might be necessary to do this daily. If the solution becomes acidic, the pH can be raised again with potassium hydroxide (KOH). A variety of pH meters and colorimetic testing kits are available for checking pH levels.

You should change the nutrient solution once every two weeks when the plants are small, and once a week as the plants begin to grow rapidly. Add water daily to keep the amount of solution constant.

Temperature

Plants grow well within a limited temperature range. Temperatures that are too high or too low will result in abnormal growth and development and reduced yields. Warm-season vegetables and most flowers prefer a temperature range between 15°C and 24°C. Cold-season vegetables, such as lettuce and spinach, grow best between 10°C and 21°C.

Water

Providing water to plants is not difficult in water culture systems, but it can be a problem in aggregate systems. During the hot summer months a large tomato plant can use two litres of water per day. Therefore, aggregate systems need to be kept sufficiently moist to prevent plant roots from drying out and dying. If roots do dry out, the plants will recover slowly but production will be reduced even when proper moisture levels have been restored.

The quality of water can also be a problem in hydroponic systems.

When to transplant

When seedlings are about 1–2 cm high or have their true leaves (those resembling the plant species, instead of the ones known as 'seed leaves' which first appear), they have reached the proper stage for transplanting to your hydroponic system.

Plants that are grown in sheltered conditions are usually too tender to transplant directly into your system. They must be 'hardened off'; that is, gradually accustomed to outdoor conditions to prevent the shock checking active growth.

Oxygen
Plants cannot live without oxygen. This vital element is obtained through photosynthesis and respiration. The roots of all hydroponically grown plants need oxygen for their life processes and for best growth. When oxygen is cut off from the roots by their constant immersion in water or compaction of the substrate, roots will suffocate and die.

Excessively alkaline or salt-laden water, such as bore water, can result in a nutrient imbalance and poor plant growth. Softened water can contain harmful amounts of sodium. Water that tests high in salts (three hundred parts per million or more on the TDS meter) should not be used as it will cause a nutrient imbalance.

Oxygen

A key element to successful hydroponic growth is oxygen. This allows for respiration, and provides energy for water and nutrient uptake. In soil, oxygen is usually abundant, unless the soil is compacted; but in hydroponics, plants growing in water will quickly exhaust the supply of dissolved oxygen. A common method of supplying oxygen is to use an air stone in the nutrient reservoir.

Light

All vegetable plants and many flowers require large amounts of sunlight. Hydroponically grown vegetables, like those grown in a garden, need at least eight to ten hours of direct sunlight each day to produce well. Most artificial lights are a poor substitute for direct sunlight as they do not provide enough light intensity to produce a crop. High-intensity discharge (HID) lights, such as metal halide and high-pressure sodium lamps, can provide more than a thousand footcandles of light, and for the serious home grower these lights can be used successfully where sunlight is inadequate. However, the fixtures and lamps are expensive and might not be economically justifiable.

Plant spacing

While it is true that you can grow plants quite close together in hydroponics because they do not have to compete for available nutrients, plant density is, nonetheless, a critical factor in optimising yields. For example, for tomatoes and cucumbers, the recommended plant density is two to three plants per square metre. Plants can be grown closer together but the yield will suffer and the crop quality will be inferior to that of plants grown at the recommended plant density.

Plant support

In a garden, plant roots are surrounded by soil which supports the growing plant. In hydroponics, plants must be artificially supported, usually with string, an A-frame structure, a trellis or stakes. For large bearers, such as pumpkin, rockmelon and watermelon, some growers also support the fruit using a hair net or a stocking.

For hydroponic ground beds, the simplest and most economical support structure consists of two fence posts positioned at each end of the bed, with taut wire strung at different levels between them. In this way, plants and vines can be supported at different stages of their growth.

Another popular method of support is a high wire or cable running above the hydroponic bed, from which plants are supported using string and specially designed clamps. This method is used in a process called 'layering',

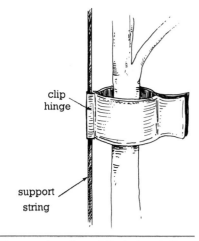

clip
hinge

support
string

Close-up view of specially designed clips to hold tall plants.

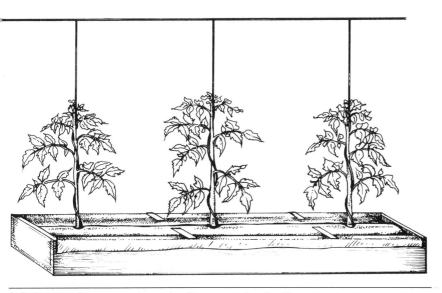

Tall plants can be supported by string from an overhead cable.

Spacing

Overcrowded plants become tangled and block each other's sun, resulting in spindly, low-yield crops. The best guide to planting distance is experience. A general rule of thumb for large plants, such as cucumbers and tomatoes, is to plant no more than three plants per square metre. For lettuce, a spacing of 250–300 mm is adequate.

whereby tomato or cucumber plants are lowered, or layered, during growth and the growing tips are supported from the cable. In this way, plant life and fruiting season can be extended to some degree. The string should be tied to the support cable directly above the plants, leaving up to one metre of extra length at the cable end in case you wish to carry the plants for a longer-than-normal growing period. They can then be lowered once they have grown as high as the cable. The clamps should be placed directly under the leaf petioles, not above them, as such a position gives no support. Clamps should not be placed under flower clusters, as the weight of maturing fruit might later break off the fruit cluster or fruit might be punctured by the clamps. For plants such as tomatoes and cucumbers, several clamps should be used for each plant, positioned every thirty or so centimetres to give adequate support as fruit matures.

These Blue Lake climbing beans are on a support frame.

Nutritional and environmental disorders

Nutritional disorders in hydroponically grown plants are caused by a deficiency or excess of at least one mineral element. Effected plants exhibit symptoms specific to the culprit element.

Mineral elements are classified as either mobile or immobile, and some are both. Mobile elements include nitrogen, potassium, phosphorus, magnesium and zinc. These can all move from their original site (older leaves) to the actively growing region of the plant (younger leaves). So, the first symptoms of a nutritional disorder will occur on the older leaves and on the lower part of the plant. Immobile elements include sulphur, calcium, iron, boron, copper and manganese. They cannot be translocated to the growing region, and so remain in the older leaves where they were originally deposited. Any deficiencies of these minerals will, therefore, first appear on the upper, younger leaves.

It is important for nutritional disorders to be recognised early; the longer a disorder continues, the faster it will spread to other areas of the plant, eventually killing plant tissue. Also, the longer a nutritional disorder continues, the more general the symptoms become and the more difficult it is to identify the disorder. General symptoms are yellowing (chlorosis) and browning (necrosis) of plant tissue.

Toxic effects in plants can be produced by both essential elements and non-essential, or trace, elements (those found in water, such as sodium, chlorine and chromium). An oversupply of essential elements is much less toxic than an oversupply of trace elements. In fact, there is a fair safety margin for excess major elements, whereas trace elements need to be precisely monitored.

An excess of one element can lead to a deficiency of another, which ultimately results in a deranged metabolism. For example, excess nitrogen or phosphorus might result in insufficient potassium; and excess potassium might lead to a deficiency of magnesium or calcium. This type of injury applies particularly to essential nutrients.

The shortage of one element can also upset a plant's ability to accumulate one or more other elements, resulting in a simultaneous mineral deficiency and surplus. For example, a shortage of boron can cause a calcium deficiency and a calcium deficiency can lead to a potassium deficiency, and vice versa. Because of these complex chain reactions it is extremely difficult to determine visually which elements are responsible for which symptoms, and early diagnosis is essential.

To increase your chances of recognising potential nutritional disorders, it is a good idea to plant alongside the main crop an 'early indicator' plant — one that is susceptible to various nutritional disorders. For example, if your

Severe marginal and interveinal chlorosis indicates an iron deficiency.

main crop is tomato, plant a passionfruit, cucumber or lettuce as well, as these plants are very susceptible, respectively, to boron, calcium and magnesium deficiencies. Such early warnings will enable you to adjust the nutrient solution in order to prevent a deficiency in the main crop. Also, a weak tomato plant will show deficiency symptoms before a strong tomato plant, acting as a further warning.

Overall, every possible tactic should be employed to give early warning of nutritional disorders, since such maladies will lead to yield reductions, poor-quality fruit, and plant death.

Generally, nutritional disorders appear simultaneously on all plants of one crop and from the bottom leaves up. (If a disorder is non-nutritional — that is, caused by pests and diseases — symptoms begin on a few plants and progress to neighbouring ones.)

Symptoms of distress in plants can sometimes be caused by environmental problems. The possibility of nutritional problems must therefore be considered in relation to all the conditions in which the plants are growing, and not merely in terms of the elements in the nutrient solution. For example, plants will not grow to their optimum capacity if the temperature is too low and might be injured if it is too high. Similarly, light is obviously important; plants will not grow well in insufficient light. The humidity of the atmosphere has a significant effect on plant growth, as water loss from the leaves is a major factor in balancing the plant's moisture requirements.

The problems of such influences in the plant environment are complicated by the fact that, rather than act independently, they modify one another. A plant's need for different elements can be affected by conditions of light, temperature and water supply, and by other factors in the general environment. For example, a plant will probably need less nitrogen but more potassium under conditions of relatively low light intensity, a fact of some significance for tomatoes grown in a glasshouse. The relationship between nitrogen and light can be demonstrated by growing a plant under normal light conditions with insufficient nitrogen: the leaves will show the well-known symptom of a nitrogen deficiency — a pale green, yellowish colour with orange and red tints. If such a plant is then shaded, the leaves will turn a darker green and growth will increase visibly.

Similarly, the rate of water absorption is less at low temperatures than at higher temperatures, and efficient intake also depends on good aeration. These facts can cause a water deficit in plants growing in cold conditions when the air temperature is high.

When plants are grown in an unsuitable environment, including one of inappropriate nutrition, they react in specific ways. Thus, if there is insufficient light, leaves will lack green colouring and might even tend towards white. Plants might be spindly and strained. If the temperature is too high, growth might be restricted, the tissue woody, and the leaves a bluish colour.

Remedial action

Deficiencies or excesses of mineral elements in hydroponically grown plants show in a number of ways: in the colour, density, size and shape of leaves; in the thickness and colour of stems and the length of internodes; in the colour, fibrousness and thickness of roots; in the abundance and timing of flowers; and in the size, colour, hardness and flavour of fruit. Recognising these particular effects is the key to diagnosing nutritional disorders.

When you recognise, or even suspect, a nutritional disorder, the first step is to replace the hydroponic nutrient solution with a fresh solution. If you have identified a malady as a nutrient deficiency, you can apply an appropri-

Potassium deficiency
A potassium deficiency can be recognised by dead areas on leaves. Excess potassium can cause magnesium deficiency and even manganese, zinc or iron deficiencies.

Phosphorus deficiency
A phosphorus deficiency stunts plants, and often turns them dark green. Maturity is often delayed.

Nitrogen deficiency
A nitrogen deficiency restricts growth and plants are generally yellow, especially on older leaves. Younger leaves might remain green while stems, petioles and lower leaf surfaces turn purple.

Tip burn
Tip burn can be attributed to a calcium deficiency or high temperatures.

Deficiency symptoms

While symptoms vary from plant to plant, the general symptoms of nutrient deficiencies can be listed as follows.

ELEMENT	SYMPTOMS
Nitrogen	Chlorosis (yellowing) of the whole plant, often with reddening. The older leaves are usually affected first.
Phosphorus	Dark green foliage, reddening or purpling of leaves or petioles.
Potassium	Older leaves might show necrotic spots or marginal burn. Younger leaves might develop red pigmentation or become interveinally chlorotic and show a shiny surface.
Sulphur	Chlorosis of the whole plant. The younger leaves are often affected first.
Magnesium	Marginal or interveinal chlorosis, often quite strongly coloured. Green area of the leaf might form an 'arrowhead' in woody plants. Strong reddening might border the chlorotic zone, usually on older tissue first. Leaf tips and margins are often turned or cupped upwards.
Calcium	The growing point dies. In fruit crops specific disorders are unique to individual fruits; for example, bitter pit in pome fruit, and blossom-end rot in tomatoes and peppers. In leaf crops, such as lettuce, tip burn can be seen.
Iron	Interveinal chlorosis. In severe cases total bleaching of young foliage is visible, followed by necrosis. Symptoms occur on young leaves first.
Chlorine	Chlorosis followed by necrosis evident with wilting leaves. Leaf tip and margin burn can also occur. Roots might appear stunted and tend to thicken near the tips.
Manganese	Interveinal chlorosis. When the condition is severe, necrotic spots or streaks might form. Initially, such symptoms often occur on middle leaves.
Boron	Death of growing points. Auxiliary buds might burst, giving a witch's-broom appearance. Some species, such as grape, might show leaf distortion. Fruit might be distorted or show woody pits or cracking of the surface. Petiole cracking in celery and hollowness in some root vegetable species are also apparent.
Zinc	Symptoms include small leaves and rosetting. In less severe cases, chlorotic mottle is apparent.
Copper	Death of young leaves. Other symptoms include chlorosis and failure of fertilisation and fruit set. (S-shaped shoot growth and fruit gumming is apparent in citrus.)
Molybdenum	In legumes general pallor is apparent. In non-legumes a mottled pale appearance is evident. In mature leaves there is marginal burn (rockmelon, maize and sunflowers). Whiptail is apparent in cauliflowers.

Toxicity symptoms

Symptoms of toxicities are generally apparent in the older leaves of plants. Many toxicities produce chlorosis and necrosis of the margins and tips. (Symptoms are also given for fluorine and aluminium since these elements are often found in water supplies.)

ELEMENT	SYMPTOMS
Nitrogen (Nitrate)	Edge burn might be followed by interveinal collapse. The root system is also restricted. In the case of ammonium-nitrogen, there is initial chlorosis, and blackening around tips and edges of leaves, and roots might die.
Phosphorus	Interveinal chlorosis is evident in younger leaves and can resemble an iron deficiency. Necrosis and tip die-back might follow in susceptible plant species. Marginal scorch and shedding of older leaves.
Potassium	Symptoms might seem similar to those of magnesium deficiency. Possible manganese, zinc and iron deficiency.
Sulphur	A reduction in growth and leaf size. Occasional interveinal chlorosis or leaf burning.
Magnesium	No visible symptoms have been noted.
Calcium	No consistent visible symptoms have been noted.
Iron	Sometimes brown spots are apparent.
Chlorine	Bronzing, chlorosis and marginal burn. Leaf drop might be premature. In some plants the marginal burn is accompanied by upward cupping or curling.
Manganese	Chlorosis, beginning at the leaf edge of older leaves, sometimes with an upward cupping. Interveinal bronze-yellow chlorosis in beans; orange-yellow marginal and interveinal chlorosis in lemons; brown tar spots in orange leaves; and necrosis in apple bark.
Boron	Interveinal necrosis, often spotty at first.
Zinc	Excess zinc produces iron chlorosis in plants.
Copper	Reduced growth followed by symptoms for iron chlorosis. Stunting and reduced branching are sometimes apparent.
Molybdenum	Symptoms are rarely observed. Tomato leaves turn golden yellow. Cauliflower seedlings turn bright purple.
Fluorine	Scorching of leaf tip and margin, extending into interveinal areas.
Aluminium	Symptoms in shoots are frequently similar to those for a phosphorus deficiency, indicating an impairment of phosphorus absorption and metabolism by high levels of aluminium. Roots grown in high concentrations of aluminium are frequently short, with many short laterals. Root tips are commonly brown.

ate foliar spray for rapid response, but take care not to burn plants by using too high a concentration. It is best to foliar feed a few plants first and then observe the results over several days before treating the whole crop. You might need to wait seven to ten days for an obvious response to a control or remedial measure.

In the event of nutrient excess (or toxicity), flush the medium with a fresh batch of nutrient solution to reduce residual salt levels. You might need to do this several times over a week or so, depending upon the severity of the disorder. Do not use water to flush the medium; flushing with fresh water can shock plant membranes and starve plants of essential elements.

ABOVE: These strawberry plants show phosphorus deficiency. The 'gooseberry-foliage' effect is indicated by dull purple tints on the leaves, which turn red as the deficiency becomes more severe.

LEFT: This crop of zucchinis is growing in a roof-top NFT system, where the natural incline of the garage roofing suits the fall of the nutrient film down the channel. The early signs of an iron deficiency are now evident. In severe cases, chlorosis of the leaves occurs, beginning as interveinal chlorosis or chlorotic mottling.

BELOW: Tip burn is now evident in this lettuce crop. Tip burn can be caused by a calcium deficiency, or high temperatures. It can be easily recognised by the inner leaf margins curling forward with a scorched appearance. In root vegetables, a calcium deficiency can be recognised at the roots which are forked and/or bent.

Cos lettuce grown in a 1.5-metre by 4-channel NFT system. This water-culture technique provides a thin film or trickle of nutrients from which plants draw their nourishment. The nutrient solution is collected in a central reservoir and then recirculated. In this particular system, the channel has removable lids which allow easy access for cleaning between crops.

This hydroponic sand bed is 6 metres long and 1.5 metres wide and is constructed of concrete reinforcement wire bent up at the sides and covered with a double layer of black plastic to contain the nutrients. The crop is mustard lettuce which is well suited to tropical climates. The seedlings are irrigated by a single 13-mm black micro-irrigation line fitted with 4-mm spaghetti tubing.

Managing diseases and pests

Disease control

Infectious diseases can be the nemesis of any gardener. Many cannot be eradicated and at best can only be contained, so prevention plays an important role. While disease problems are rarer in hydroponics than in soil gardening, diseases still pose a serious threat to plants if allowed to go uncontrolled. With ever-increasing awareness of the dangers of chemical treatments, home gardeners should therefore maintain a strict sanitation program to prevent and control the spread of diseases.

Even with the best preventative programme, disease organisms can still get a foothold in any hydroponic crop. Such pathogens can be transmitted from the bottom of a seedling tray or pot via water, or they might simply appear on purchased seedlings or cuttings. While some rely on the moisture of the plant foliage to develop, others need a very wet root medium. Some diseases, such as the rusts and Botrytis, produce wind-borne spores which can be transported through the air from host plants near or far.

Hydroponic gardeners should check their crops daily for disease, just as they do for insects and changes in the nutrient solution, so that early identification can be made and controls implemented.

The diseases that afflict hydroponic crops are caused by four groups of organisms — viruses, bacteria, fungi and nematodes. In order to control pathogens it is important to understand the characteristics and life cycles of each of these.

Viruses

Viruses are minute organisms that live within plant and animal cells and cause numerous abnormalities. Plants do not produce antibodies, which means that they neither recover from a virus infection nor develop immunity, although resistance to some viruses can be bred into commercial crop varieties.

No pesticides are available to combat viral disease; once a plant becomes infected it will remain infected for life, even though the symptoms might become masked or the plant might 'grow out of it' under certain conditions. If an infected plant is allowed to stay in the system, the virus might be carried from plant to plant. The disease can only be eliminated by removing and destroying the infected plant.

The most recognisable symptom of viral diseases is deformity, stunting and dwarfing. However, leaves often show the first symptoms. In vegetable crops the most common symptom is a change in colour. Leaves might show spots, streaks, blotches, or rings of light green, yellow, white, brown or black. The leaves can also change their shape or size, sometimes puckering

Pests and diseases

In hydroponics, soil-borne pests and diseases are virtually eliminated. Nonetheless, plants grown in soilless culture are still susceptible to certain common pests and diseases. Vigilance and early identification are important in controlling such problems. The key to a healthy garden is cleanliness, favourable environmental conditions and proper cultural practices.

Bacteria prevention

The best prevention against bacteria is to eliminate infected plants and to sterilise pots, containers, channel and irrigation equipment. Between crops, systems should be thoroughly cleaned using a mild solution of chlorine which is commonly available in household bleach (sodium-hypochlorite). After cleaning, the system should be thoroughly flushed with fresh water before replanting.

Fungi prevention

The best control against fungi is proper sanitation, getting rid of diseased plants and using resistant varieties. Among the least harmful chemicals that can be used in combating fungi are sulphur and copper. Sulphur is considered the least objectionable among organic and hydroponic gardeners.

or developing rolled margins. Flowers will appear dwarfed, deformed, streaked or faded, even changing into leafy structures. These are only a few of the symptoms of viral infections.

Viral infections are generally not transmitted through seeds. However, a crop can suffer serious loss if a virus is transmitted to seedlings early and spreads efficiently. While viruses can spread unaided from cell to cell in one plant, they require active assistance to pass from one plant to another. A virus usually spreads as a result of insects feeding on an infected plant then a healthy one. It can also be transmitted by grafting and sometimes by secateurs that have been used on an infected plant.

Bacteria

Bacteria are single-cell micro-organisms that are difficult to control. Although a few bactericides are available, control is primarily through prevention, and elimination of infected plants. Some of the more common bacterial diseases include bacterial wilt (*Pseudomonas caryophylli*), known to affect carnations; bacterial blight (*Xanthomonas pelargoni*), also known as stem rot and leaf spot, on pelargoniums; soft rot (*Erwinia chrysanthemi*) of cuttings and bulbs; bacterial leaf spots (*Xanthomonas hederae*), common on geraniums and English ivy; and crown gall (*Agrobacterium tumefasciens*) which infects roses, chrysanthemums and geraniums.

Fungi

Fungal diseases are the most common of the four groups and have been the downfall of many a home gardener. However, they are the easiest to diagnose, and lend themselves to control measures.

Fungi are much more complex than bacteria, being multicellular organisms often consisting of several tissues. Most fungi reproduce asexually by the formation of spores.

The most easily recognised fungus is powdery mildew, characterised by a whitish powder on the surface of leaves, stems and sometimes petals. Mildew spores are easily detached from the plants and carried along by the wind to surrounding plants where they initiate new infections.

High humidity is conducive to this disease, so ventilation and heating in backyard greenhouses should be adjusted to avoid high-humidity conditions.

To control mildew you will need to grow resistant varieties and use fungicides, both outdoors and indoors. Although recommendations change, fungicides containing sulphur will always be on the list. Dusting sulphurs can be applied quickly and easily. As a preventative measure, crops should be treated with sulphur powders or sprays at regular intervals. But beware of sulphur in summer and under greenhouse conditions, as it causes defoliation under high temperatures.

Botrytis (*Botrytis cinerea*) is a common grey-mould fungus which attacks a variety of ornamental plants, causing more losses than any other single pathogen. Symptoms include a soft rot and conspicuous grey mould on older dead tissue. The fungus attacks stems and petals on carnations, chrysanthemums, roses, azaleas and geraniums. It is usually identified by the development of fuzzy, greyish spore masses over the surface of the rotted tissues, although such spores will not develop under dry conditions. Spores are readily dislodged and carried by the wind to new plants. However, the spores will germinate and produce new infections only when in contact with water, whether from splashing, condensation or exudation, and then only on petals or injured tissue.

Again, high humidity favours Botrytis and should be countered with adequate ventilation to prevent spore production. In greenhouse or indoor environments avoid splashing and condensation on plant surfaces. Because the fungus readily attacks old or dead tissues, and produces large quantities of airborne spores, strict sanitation cannot be over-emphasised. Fungicides can be used to control the disease, although a high degree of control without modification to the environment is difficult.

Root-rot diseases, such as *Rhizoctonia* and *Pythium*, not only cause damping off of seedlings but, together with *Thielaviopsis* and *Colletotrichum*, cause root and basal stem rot of older plants. These fungi are common and attack a wide range of plants. Both spread by mechanical transfer of mycelium or spores in infested media, plant tissue or nutrient solutions.

Symptoms of *Pythium* are a wet rot that makes roots look hollow and collapsed. It is favoured by cool, wet conditions. *Rhizoctonia* causes a drier brown rot and is favoured by an intermediate range of moisture, neither too wet nor too dry. It is also favoured by high temperatures, but this is not always so. *Thielaviopsis* causes a drier lesion than *Rhizoctonia*, but one that soon turns black because of the large number of black spores produced by the fungus in the lesion. The disease does not occur in pH conditions between pH 4.5 and 5.0. *Colletotrichum* is often associated with root decay in NFT systems and can invade healthy tissue.

Preventative measures are the same for all root-rot diseases. The most effective controls are the use of well-drained mediums; thorough disinfection or pasteurisation of the medium, and sterilisation of installations, including seedling trays, pots, tools and benches; clean plants; and a sound sanitation programme. Fungicides can also be added to hydroponic solutions.

Verticillium diseases affect a wide variety of ornamental plants, including chrysanthemums, snapdragons, roses, geraniums and begonias. Symptoms vary with the host. With chrysanthemums marginal wilting of the leaves usually occurs, followed by chlorosis and eventually death and browning of the leaves. Symptoms occur only after blossom buds have formed. Snapdragons can seem completely healthy until blossoms appear, at which time the foliage suddenly wilts. Rose buds tend to turn blue and fail to open, and leaves and stem tissue become mottled before the leaves fall and the stem dies. In the case of begonias, yellowing usually occurs on the leaf margins, but the most distinctive symptom is the development of an extremely shiny lower leaf surface. Like other preventative measures for fungi, installations and implements should be sterilised between crops, and cuttings or seedlings should be purchased from reliable nurseries. *Verticillium*, however, is seldom a problem in well-run hydroponic systems.

Nematodes

Nematodes, also called eelworms, are parasites that live in plants, soil, hydroponic mediums or fresh water. They are bilaterally symmetrical, elongated, usually tapered at both ends, and almost invisible to the unaided eye. Most nematodes are not harmful and contribute to the ecological balance of soil. However, a few are harmful, especially when large populations occur, resulting in crop injuries. The most effective means of eradicating nematodes is by pasteurising the hydroponic medium and sterilising all equipment.

Harmful nematodes can be grouped into two broad categories — those that feed on roots, and those that feed on buds and leaves. Root knot nematodes are among the most common plant-damaging types. Infected plants usually appear stunted and tend to wilt on warmer days. Root galls are generally conspicuous and easily recognised. However, the presence of galls does not necessarily lead to crop loss. With adequate nutrients, infected plants will continue to grow well and produce almost normally.

Plants infected with root nematodes should be removed and discarded so that the disease doesn't spread. Thoroughly pasteurise mediums and installations before planting the next crop.

Nematode prevention
The best control against nematodes is to discard infected plants and to sterilise the substrate before replanting. If in doubt, discard and replace the substrate.

Leaf and bud nematodes can cause leaf or fruit distortion on many ornamentals and strawberries. Leaf nematodes cause leaf spots and defoliation. Yellow or brown spots appear first on the lower leaves, which eventually turn black. With favourable temperature and moisture conditions, the spotting spreads until most of the leaf is destroyed. Leaf nematodes can be effectively controlled by chemicals applied to the foliage.

Ask your supplier for the appropriate product.

Disease prevention

Disease can be prevented by means of a total programme of sanitation. Diseases caused by organisms such as Botrytis need 'free' water on the plant surface for spores to germinate. Free water often occurs as condensation, with warm air holding more moisture than cold air. During warm days the air picks up more moisture, and at night the air cools and its moisture capacity drops until the dew point is reached and water begins to condense on any solid surface.

In a greenhouse environment, condensation can be controlled by three methods: adequate ventilation (or exhaust fans at a low capacity), circulating air around the environment with the use of an oscillating fan, or totally extracting the air at regular intervals.

Mildew is also encouraged by high humidity. This can be controlled to some degree by ventilating at regular intervals and maintaining good air circulation. Humidity can be further reduced by watering early in the day when warm air can absorb moisture from wet surfaces.

Root-rot and damping-off diseases are conveyed by mechanical transfer of the fungus into the root media. Automatic watering helps to prevent this occurrence because it minimises the splashing which can occur during hand watering. Good drainage of the medium also helps since infection by many pathogens is enhanced by high root-medium moisture levels. It is essential to avoid waterlogging of the root zone at any stage.

Other control measures include sterilising trays, pots and other containers before they come into contact with a clean medium. You should also sterilise tools, plastic supports and watering systems.

Ensure that plant debris is removed and safely disposed of. Disposal points should be sealed and far enough away for micro-organisms, wind-blown spores and insects to be unable to make their way back to the main crop. Never throw plant debris on the floor during pruning as pathogens can easily spread to other plants. Rather, make a cloth pouch that can be carried around your waist. Always make the effort to walk the extra metre for disease prevention. Devise a system that follows sound principles of sanitation without causing too much extra effort.

Finally, when you are purchasing plant stock from a nursery, you are depending on the sanitation programme of a business. Select your plant sources carefully and inspect each plant for disease. If propagating your own stock, maintain a careful disease prevention programme. Inspect your stock regularly, use only sterilised implements when taking cuttings, and transport plant material in clean containers.

Pest control

Insects, mites and other related animal pests pose an ever-present threat to the quality of hydroponic crops. A careful plan of prevention and control should therefore be maintained. While a number of effective chemical sprays are available to combat insect infestations, hydroponic gardeners tend to

Disease prevention

- Purchase disease-free plants from reputable nurseries.
- Periodically sterilise hydroponic tools and equipment.
- Remove all plant debris such as pinched-off plant tops and superfluous buds from the growing area.
- Maintain proper watering practices to minimise free water on plants.

ignore these in preference to biological and organic controls. After all, using chemical sprays defeats many gardeners' purpose in adopting hydroponic techniques in the first place.

Eradicating pests by using chemical sprays can also have serious consequences for the ecosystem. Although many of us would prefer to have no insects in our gardens, the inescapable truth is that we need them to maintain the ecological balance. While 'bad' bugs can wreak havoc, there are also many 'good' insects in the garden, and chemical sprays are not discerning in what they eradicate. In the normal scheme of things, the good and bad bugs balance each other in the food chain. However, insect populations can get out of balance occasionally, and we do need to take some kind of control action. Such action does not mean elimination or eradication, but rather reducing infestations within a tolerable range.

Insects can be brought into the garden in a variety of ways, plant stock purchased from the local nursery being a common entry point. Such plants should be inspected carefully for insects and, if affected, should not be brought into your garden. Insects can also be attracted from neighbouring gardens by scents or simply carried in by the wind. It is inevitable that insects are going to get into your garden, but if the harmful bugs can be detected early, they can be controlled before any significant damage is done.

Insects usually establish themselves in a particular location, perhaps a warm temperature zone or a wind-sheltered area, and exhibit particular plant preferences. When doing the rounds of the garden, you should identify such areas and plants and inspect them regularly, with particular emphasis on the undersides of leaves. Some insects, such as slugs, will hide in damp and dark spaces, or attach themselves to the underside of leaves on the surface on the medium, coming out at night to feed on the upper plant. One must be aware of these hiding places, and know the signs of the pest.

Spider mites, also called two-spotted mites and red spider mites, are the bane of many a hydroponic gardener. This tiny pest is virtually invisible to the naked eye, and is identifiable only by the damage it does. Early symptoms of its presence can be seen when your plants start showing little yellow speckles on the leaf surface. If you look on the underside of the leaf you might see very tiny, oval-shaped mites scurrying about. A fine web over the plant tops is another early warning indicator, and this can be revealed by spraying your plant tops with a fine mist of water (the drops will cling to the web). In spite of efforts to rid your garden of spider mite, they can be transmitted on your clothes or just float in on wind currents.

Spider mites are most prevalent during hot, dry months. During the winter months, they stop feeding and laying, and crawl off to protected nooks and crannies where they hibernate until spring. Each generation takes about two weeks from egg to adult. At temperatures below 10°C they become dormant, and at temperatures above 29°C their life cycle accelerates. Since they dislike wet conditions, raising the humidity level in a controlled environment is beneficial. For outdoor gardens, plants should be sprayed with water regularly.

Whitefly is a common pest and is easily recognised by its waxy white, moth-like appearance. With a wingspan of about 3 mm, whitefly is usually found on the underside of leaves where it sucks sap from the plant. When disturbed, colonies of whitefly will rush out in the air, hesitate a while, then fly back into the foliage. Heavily infested plants will yellow and grow poorly.

For heavy whitefly infestations, the most effective control is whitefly parasites (*Encarsia formosa*) which kill the pest before it hatches. The parasite works by laying its eggs inside the whitefly eggs, so that another parasite

Insect control
Insect free hydroponic gardens depend upon creating a balance among the insect population. Ideally, beneficial predators and parasites keep the numbers of potential pests at a low, tolerable level, therefore making sprays, dusts and traps unnecessary.

Preventing insect problems
There is much you can do to prevent problems with insects. Healthy plants can withstand infestations better than weak plants. A well-balanced diet of nutrients will help to maintain healthy plants.

Plants need nitrogen, but an overdose has been found to make plants overly succulent and therefore encourage various sucking insects. It is best to make nitrogen available to plants slowly, by using well-balanced hydroponic nutrients.

Dragonflies are garden friends. Their larvae feed on water-borne pests such as mosquito larvae.

The praying mantis eats many garden insect pests.

Lacewing not only look beautiful, but are extremely helpful in the garden — their larvae eat huge numbers of aphids.

hatches out instead of a whitefly. Another natural control is the use of yellow sticky traps.

Aphids are a serious threat to all gardens. What you notice first are leaves that are curled, puckered and discoloured. On closer inspection dense colonies of tiny, soft-bodied, pear-shaped insects can be seen, especially on the tender growing tips and underneath leaves.

Compared to most insects, aphids move quite slowly when disturbed. They come in almost any colour and feed by sucking on plant juices. While that in itself is serious, the most serious threat is the diseases they carry. Aphids also produce a shiny honeydew which accumulates into a choking mould. Combine these problems with the fact that aphids are born already pregnant, they're all female, and they reach adulthood in one week, and you realise why an aphid strike can be devastating. The natural controls against aphids are ladybirds and green lacewings. Between these two good bugs, aphid control is usually quite successful.

Ways to control insect pests

The two non-chemical means of insect prevention and control are biological and organic.

Biological control simply means using living organisms which feed on other insects; or handpicking or companion planting, whereby one plant protects another because of the odours it emits, or the taste of its foliage. Other biological controls can be microbials — organisms that make insects sick — or parasites that feed on insects from the inside.

Organic control means the use of non-chemical concoctions, usually made from recipes handed down from one generation to another. Other organic controls include crop rotation to disrupt an insect's habitat and hence breeding cycle, and the use of simple-yet-effective sticky traps.

Natural predators

For many home gardeners, natural predators are the first line of defence. The main natural predators are ladybird (*Crytolaemus montrouzieri*), praying mantis (*Tenodera sinensis*), lacewing (*Chrysopa carnea*), predatory mite (*Phytoseiulus persimilis*), parasitic wasps (*Leptomastix dactylopii*), and scale insect predators (*Chilocorus lophanthae, — circumdatus* and — *baileyii*).

These can be purchased from your local hydroponic centre, or collected from surrounding bushlands and gardens and transported back to your garden. You don't have to worry about these insects becoming pests themselves as they are carnivorous (they do not like plants) and they can't harm people or pets in any way. Most are so small that you are hardly aware of them, and when the pest populations die off, they will too.

Ladybirds are predatory, both as adults and as larvae. They prey on a variety of pests such as aphid, scale insects, mealy bug, thrip, small caterpillars and mites. The black ladybug (*Cryptolaemus montrouzeri*) is of Australian origin and one of the oldest and most successful biological controls. In the early 1900s it was used to save the southern Californian citrus crop from mealy bug. It has a large appetite and one to four ladybirds are enough for one infested plant. The ladybird eats not only mealy bug, but aphid and scale.

Praying mantis are long, narrow, carnivorous insects. Their name stems from their habit of sitting motionless with their forelegs raised and held together as though they were praying. In fact, they are more likely to be waiting for their prey!

Praying mantis eggs are attached to vegetation and are variable in form. Each species produces a characteristically shaped ootheca which looks like a small barrel with a lid. Mantis are among the most popular pest controls and a garden 'fun pet'. They are very interesting to watch and can even be enticed to eat bits of food.

Lacewing larvae are 'walking garbage bins', eating a vast variety of insects smaller than themselves, as well as each other. Sometimes known as 'aphid-lions', they can consume 500 to 2000 aphids or other pests during their 3–6-week life.

Lacewing eggs are laid on the tip of individual stalks of stiff silk. Adult lacewings often fly to lighted windows or bulbs. If you are careful, you can collect them in a container and transfer them to your garden. Specimens should be kept apart as they might eat each other.

A number of **parasitic wasps** in Australia play a predatory role — amongst them the true wasp, digger wasp, chalcid wasp and aphid wasp, which are of interest to gardeners. The aphid wasp is very small (3–5 mm long) and brown or black. It is an important parasite of aphids, scale insects and mealy bugs. The chalcid wasp will lay its eggs in the eggs of other insects. When the larval wasp hatches, it eats the tissue of its host. These wasps can be recognised by their beautiful blue-and-green metallic bodies. They are among the smallest of all insects and can be easily recognised because they have no 'waist' between thorax and abdomen.

Predatory mite, also known as the Chilean mite, the predatory mite has been used to control spider mite in a wide range of greenhouse and outdoor crops in Australia and overseas. It is an extremely voracious and effective predator, and quite often completely eliminates the population of the pest it consumes.

Lacewing eggs are usually found under a leaf, attached to stalks by stiff silk.

Biological controls

If a crop is endangered despite your precautions, you should first consider biological controls. While most gardeners are familiar with the predaceous ladybug and praying mantis, many lesser known beneficial insects and even pathogens deserve recognition as effective natural controls.

Predator	Pest controlled
Ladybird	Aphid, mealy bug, citrus mealy bug, mealy bug eggs.
Praying mantis	Most insects
Lacewing	Aphid, citrus mealy bug, spider mite, thrip and many worm eggs.
Predatory mite	Spider mite
Parasitic wasps	Citrus mealy bug
Scale predators	Scale insects

Organic sprays

The most popular organic sprays are insecticidal soaps, which create a very thin film on plant leaves and block the fine tubes that all insects breathe through. However, the soap has no other effect and regular treatment is required. For best results, you need to spray directly onto the insect and to cover the undersides of leaves thoroughly. Since soap sprays can also adversely affect 'good' bugs, it is best to use this strategy as spot spraying. These soaps are mild and will not burn plants.

Another effective organic control is kelp, used as a foliar spray. Available in powdered form, kelp is providing effective control against a wide variety of insects, but particularly against red spider mite. Kelp is not only harmless

Plant repellent	Insect
Mint, sage, rosemary	Cabbage worm
Onion, garlic	Spider mite
Radish	Stink bug
Marigold	Tomato hornworm, thrip
Marigold, nasturtium	Whitefly
Geranium	Leaf hopper
Spearmint, tansy, pennyroyal	Ants

Traps and barriers

After biological controls have failed to stem an insect strike, and before turning to sprays and dusts, consider trapping the enemy. One of the most popular traps is nothing more than a shallow dish or jar lid containing some stale beer. Snails and slugs will drown in the stuff at night. Or alternatively, a perimeter of wood ash scattered around the bases of plants will block many crawling and walking insects.

Algae

In the scheme of things, algae may play a surprising role in the growth of plants — it may add organic matter to the nutrient solution. However, it is also known to rob the solution of precious oxygen and minerals.

but also beneficial to plant health. The only disadvantage is that it can stain plant foliage if used in too high a concentration.

Some very good home-made insecticidal recipes have been handed down over time. One such recipe is to dissolve a two-centimetre cube of pure soap in a saucepan of hot water, adding a crushed clove of garlic, and an onion or a few hot peppers, finely chopped or juiced, or cayenne pepper. Once blended, add cold water to make four litres of working solution.

Companion planting

Companion planting means mixing plants in a row so that those with unpleasant odours, tastes or other characteristics repel the pests from the host plants that they like and damage. Generally, insects find the mix of plants not to their liking and leave the garden for better feeding grounds. Finding which plants work best for interplanting is a matter of trial and error, but the list in the side column will be helpful for hydroponic crops.

Sticky traps

Sticky traps are closely related to companion planting in that they confuse, lure or trap pests. However, such traps can also catch beneficial insects such as lacewing. Therefore, only special sticky traps should be used, ones that have been specifically designed for certain insects. These traps use floral or plant scents or specific sexual scents from specific insects to lure pests. Some traps are also made with certain attractive colours, such as yellow which is renowned for attracting whiteflies.

When insect infestations occur, it is sometimes necessary to implement a number of strategies in close succession. For home gardeners, an effective management plan to keep in mind is to:
• identify pest insects, and know their natural enemies
• monitor insect populations with sticky traps
• determine the level of plant injury
• if the population is above acceptable levels, use one or more control strategies
• evaluate the effect of the strategy

Algae control

Algae is a common occurrence in hydroponic systems. It can be unsightly and, on drying, it can emit a foul odour. It will also rob the nutrient solution of minute elements, including oxygen, but not enough to cause alarm. Contrary to popular belief, algae is not harmful to your plants, except on rare occasions in stagnant water when it can harbour insects and diseases. Some people will even argue that algae gives off certain enzymes which are beneficial to your plants, and they openly encourage its growth.

Algae requires two things to flourish: light and oxygen. If one or the other is not present, algae will not grow. In hydroponics, algae growth can be limited or excluded by ensuring that channels and pipes are light proof. For open hydroponic systems that use a growing substrate, black/white plastic film can be cut to size and placed over the growing container so that light cannot reach the medium. The best way to prevent algae growth is to block light from the nutrient reservoir with a lid, some plastic film or a hessian bag. Between crops, all containers, channels or pipes, irrigation lines and the nutrient reservoir should be thoroughly flushed with a mild solution of chlorine or ordinary household bleach.

Maintaining your system

The good running order of your hydroponic system, and hence the quality and quantity of the produce, depends upon a sound maintenance and management programme. Each day about 5–10 minutes should be set aside to inspect your hydroponic system for any problems, such as system blockages, 'pooling' or 'puddling'; equipment fatigue or failure; insect infestations; or the early signs of plant disease or plant malnutrition.

A common problem with an NFT system is nutrient-flow blockage. This can be caused by a blocked filter, algae growth in micro-irrigation lines, or a root system growing into channel outlets. Depending upon the size of the channel in use, and the type of plant being cultivated, plant roots may sometimes need to be trimmed to prevent 'pooling'. This is where the nutrient solution forms pools between plants owing to large root structures within the channel, thus preventing the normal flow of the nutrient film. Excessive pooling may cause root rot and plant death.

Systems that use fine sand as the growing substrate should be checked daily to ensure that 'puddling' does not occur. A typical example of puddling can be seen on a beach by watching footstep impressions on the sand near the water's edge. Water quickly rises from below to form a puddle. In hydroponics, puddling causes plant roots to be constantly immersed in the nutrient solution which may cause plant death. To avoid puddling ensure your substrate drains well. Drainage can be improved by mixing coarse sand or gravel with the fine sand.

At the end of the growing season, or between crops, the hydroponic system should be thoroughly stripped and cleaned using a hard scrubber and a mild solution of chlorine, or household bleach. Ensure that all the irrigation lines are also cleaned. After circulating the cleaning solution through the system for up to two hours, empty the solution, drain the reservoir and flush the system again using fresh, clean water. Once you are satisfied your system is clean, you should then ensure the pump is serviced, and the filter either cleaned or replaced.

Care should also be taken with test equipment such as digital pH and EC meters. These instruments are designed to provide you and years of accurate testing and control of the pH and concentration of the nutrient solution in your hydroponic system.

Maximise your growth

In recirculating hydroponic systems the growing plants feed on selected nutrients in the solution. When the nutrients are used by the growing plants this depletes

Submerged meters

Electronic meters are not waterproof. In the case of pocket meters, they are designed to be immersed only to around one-third of their depth. If the worst happens and you drop your meter into the nutrient solution, don't panic. If you act promptly, there need be little or no damage to it.

On recovering your meter, open the top and take out the small battery module. Remove and dry the batteries. Turn the meter upside down to drain any water. Pour in a teaspoon of methylated spirits, shake and drain. Do this again. As soon as possible, take the meter to a service station and blow out any remaining water with compressed air.

Once it is dry, spray a lubricant, such as WD-40 or equivalent, on a soft cloth, wipe the batteries and replace them, making sure that they are inserted the right way. If you have acted promptly, your meter should have suffered little or no damage, and will now be back in working order.

the concentration of the overall nutrient solution, and changes the pH. Left without adjustment, the nutrients in the solution will be used up until the solution is almost pure water. Hence, to maintain maximum growth, the nutrient solution needs to be maintained at its optimal strength.

If the plants remove acidic nutrients, the solution becomes more alkaline. In the same way, if the plants use up alkaline salts, the solution will become more acidic. As the plants grow in size and pass through different stages of maturity, they require different nutrients and they require more and more nutrients to maintain their mass and growth. The concentration of the nutrient solution is adjusted by adding nutrient elements, and the pH of the solution is adjusted with acid and alkaline pH buffer solutions.

It is very easy to maximise the growth of your plants by following these three steps each day.

1 Top up the level of the nutrient tank with fresh water, and circulate for a short time to mix the water with the nutrient.

2 Test the nutrient concentration with the EC, TDS or cF meter. For most young plants the concentration should be around 500–750 parts per million, and for adult plants around 1000–1500 parts per million. Increase the nutrient concentration by adding a little at a time of the concentrated nutrient until the desired reading is reached. If the solution is too concentrated, remove some of the nutrient solution and add fresh water until the correct reading is reached.

3 Test the pH of the solution with your meter. The pH should read around 5.5 to 6.0 for most plants. If the pH is too low, add dilute 'pH raise solution' a little at a time until the desired pH is reached. If the pH is too high, add 'pH lower solution' until the desired pH is reached. Do not attempt to correct the pH balance of your nutrient solution using concentrated 'raise or lower solution' as it is too easy to overshoot the correct pH level and have to adjust the pH the other way.

Calibrating your meters

If you are using pH and electroconductivity 'pen-type' meters, they will require periodic calibration. Each meter has specific calibration solutions. A calibration solution is a laboratory-grade solution guaranteed to conform to a set pH or conductivity.

For pH meters, the typical calibration solutions are pH 7.0 and pH 4.0. The usual practice is to use the calibration solution closest to the pH of the nutrient solution. For this reason, most people use a calibration solution of around pH 7.0. For conductivity meters, a typical solution is cF 2.76 mS/cm (equivalent to a reading of 1382 parts per million).

The process of calibration is simple. Clean your meter with fresh water and then dry it. A dirty or wet meter will contaminate your calibration solution, rendering it inaccurate. Immerse the probe in the calibration solution and check the reading. If your meter is correctly calibrated, the reading should be the same as the calibration solution. For example, if you are using pH 7.0 calibration solution, the meter should read pH 7.0. If this is not the case, use a jeweller's screwdriver to turn the small calibration screw on the back of the meter until a reading of pH 7.0 is achieved. Other meters have an automatic, push-button calibration control. Conductivity meters can be calibrated in the same manner.

Keeping records

Good records are invaluable to the serious hydroponic gardener, enabling comparisons from crop to crop and from season to season. You should record any unusual observations, such as aphid strikes which affect some plants but not others, and you might even like to develop your own companion planting guide to prevent such strikes occurring in future crops.

In most cases, if a problem develops it can usually be traced back to a specific point in time. From my experience, it usually takes seven to ten days for a plant to show visible symptoms of a malady. Once again, a record of your activities might help to isolate the cause of the problem. And any corrective action you take will filter through to the plant after a further seven to ten days.

If you scale up your hydroponic activities to any significant degree you might also benefit from making a financial analysis of your hydroponic enterprise. This should take into account capital cost, operating costs, equipment repairs and maintenance, and consumables such as nutrients and agents to raise and lower pH.

If you keep a diary of all your hydroponic activities, you will probably find it useful to write up all of the data into a summary upon harvest.

Remember! By keeping good records you will be able quickly to fine tune your growing skills, and maximise the potential of your hydroponic crops.

Sample log

Crop:	Lettuce	Tomato	Parsley
Variety:	Coral	(etc.)	(etc.)
Crop duration:	5 weeks		
Growing system:	NFT		
Date planted:	1 Oct		
Date harvested:	7 Nov		
pH range:	6.5		
EC/TDS/cF range:	1mS/700 ppm		
Av. water temp:	24°C		
Planting density:	40 plants		
Yield:	34		
Est. yearly turnaround:	6 crops @ 40 = 240 lettuces		
Daily checks:	pH/EC check		
Monthly checks:	Nutrient change bi-monthly		
Comments:			

Ten common questions about hydroponics

How nutritious are hydroponically grown vegetables and fruits?

Hydroponically grown fruit and vegetables have the same nutritional values as those grown in soil, provided they are consumed soon after harvesting. The longer any produce is left before consumption, the lower its nutritional value. Therefore, produce that is grown for supermarkets, whether hydroponically or in soil, will progressively lose nutritional value as it is finding its way to the supermarket shelf and then to the consumer's table. To minimise loss of nutrition, some hydroponically grown plants are harvested and conveyed to the supermarket with the roots still attached, so that they remain fresh until purchased by the consumer.

Do hydroponically grown fruit and vegetables taste better than soil-grown produce?

Hydroponically grown fruit and vegetables taste as good as those grown in soil, provided they are grown to optimum levels. However, produce will lack flavour if cultivated outside what are considered to be the optimum growing conditions for that plant. For example, if the conductivity for a tomato plant is not kept within acceptable limits, produce will be soft and lack flavour.

Is it true that hydroponic plants mature faster than soil-grown plants?

Not all plants grow faster hydroponically. Generally, plants such as ferns and Australian natives share the same growing profile, regardless of whether they are grown in soil or hydroponics, although the latter have larger leaves and a better overall appearance. This is because they receive the full spectrum of nutrients. Hydroponically grown flowers, vegetables and fruits do grow faster — about a third faster — than those grown in soil, provided they are grown to their optimum growing conditions. This is because plants do not have to search or compete for available nutrients as they do in soil, and the environment can be manipulated to some extent.

Is it true that hydroponically grown fruit and vegetables are larger than soil-grown produce?

Generally, hydroponically grown fruit and vegetables are slightly larger in size, and, if grown to optimum growing conditions, the quality of the produce is much higher. Once again, this is because plants receive a well-balanced diet of water and nutrients.

Can all plants be grown hydroponically?

All plants can be grown hydroponically, although some plants grow better in some systems than in others. For example, lettuce and many herbs excel in water culture, and trees and shrubs grow better in large tubs or buckets. The only exception is fungi, such as mushrooms, whose nutrient requirement is completely different from that of other plants and which cannot be grown hydroponically.

Are inorganic nutrients harmful in hydroponics?

No. Hydroponically grown plants use the same inorganic elements as those that are found in soil. When compost and manures are added to soil, this matter takes time to decompose into the inorganic elements necessary for plant growth. In hydroponics, the same inorganic elements are supplied to plants directly.

How much nutrient solution do plants take up daily?

The uptake of water and nutrient depends on the demands of photosynthesis and transpiration by plants, and these factors depend on the leaf area of the plant, light intensity, light duration, air temperature, relative humidity and wind factor. For example, a plant with five times more leaf area than a younger plant of the same variety will take up approximately five times more water and nutrient under similar conditions. The same plant will have a higher uptake in hot, dry conditions than in cool, humid conditions. Also, plants grown indoors, under heavy shade or during cloudy weather will demand far less water and nutrient than if the same plants were grown in direct sunlight.

Can the growing medium be re-used?

All growing mediums can be re-used, unless there has been a root disease in the system. In this case the mediums need to be sterilised or replaced altogether.

Is algae harmful to hydroponic plants?

Wherever there is light and sufficient nutrient, algae will grow. However, in a medium system this is rarely a problem as long as the system is performing effectively. More care needs to be taken in systems that use no medium. Plant roots do not like light. If algae is growing in the channel, then it is an indication that too much light is entering the channel, and steps need to be taken to eliminate it.

Is hydroponics expensive to establish and run?

The cost of a hydroponic system depends on the degree of its automation. For most home gardeners, simple hydroponic systems can be constructed using unused materials usually found in most backyards or garages. Equipment such as pumps and timers can be adapted to most systems simply and inexpensively. Nutrients are an ongoing cost, but these are inexpensive to purchase and last for several months, depending upon the size of the hydroponic enterprise.

Is hydroponics just a trend?

No. Hydroponic techniques are now recognised as a practicable and achievable solution to the world's growing food shortages, especially in Third World countries exposed to population pressures, and in countries that lack good arable land. Compared to traditional soil farming, crop turnaround is accelerated, and pest and disease problems are reduced. From an environmental point of view, hydroponics contributes to water conservation.

Suppliers and associations

Suppliers

Accent Hydroponics Pty Ltd
89 Marigold Street, Revesby NSW 2212
Tel: (02) 772 3166

Aquaponics
Lot 12 Warton Road, Canning Vale WA 6155
Tel: (09) 45 2133

Captain Hydro
No. 1 Machinery Drive, South Tweed Heads
NSW 2486
Tel: (075) 98 3800 Fax: (075) 24 6780

Gold Coast Hydroponics
Australia Fair, Southport Qld 4215
Tel: (075) 91 6380

Green Lantern Hydroponics
188 Warrigal Road, Oakleigh Vic 3166
Tel: (03) 563 7435

Greenlite Hydroponics
76 Chapel Street, Windsor Vic 3181
Tel: (03) 510 6832 Fax: (03) 510 9483

Greenlite Hydroponics
39 Burwood Highway, Burwood Vic 3125
Tel: (03) 888 8885

Growool Horticultural Systems
2 Wiltona Place, Girraween NSW 2145
Tel: (02) 631 7007 Fax: (02) 636 8775

Growth Technology Pty Ltd
244 South Terrace, South Fremantle WA 6162
Tel: (09) 430 4713 Fax: (09) 430 6939

Homeplant Pty Ltd
PO Box 2162
North Parramatta NSW 2151
Tel: (02) 604 0469

Hydroponics Sales & Service
1 Salisbury Crescent, Colonel Light Gardens
SA 5041
Tel: (08) 272 2000

Irelands Hydroponics
31 Main Street, Kinglake Vic 3763
Tel: (057) 86 1280 Fax: (057) 86 1286

Nutriflo Hydroponics
59 Dalnott Road, Gorokan NSW 2263
Tel: (043) 92 6060

Perth Hydroponics
608 Albany Highway, Victoria Park WA 6100
Tel: (09) 361 8211 Fax: (09) 470 2036

R&D Aquaponics
Unit 4, 13–14 Hallstrom Place, Wetherill Park
NSW 2164
Tel: (02) 604 5788 Fax: (02) 609 4871

Sage Horticultural Systems
121 Herald Street, Cheltenham Vic 3192
Tel: (03) 553 3777 Fax: (03) 555 3013

Soluble Solutions
525 Military Road, Mosman NSW 2088
Tel: (02) 968 2808

South Pacific Hydroponics Pty Ltd
252 Oxford Street, Bondi Junction NSW 2022
Tel: (02) 369 3928 Fax: (02) 369 3962
Unit 2/62 Keane St
Currajong QLD 4182
Tel & Fax: (077) 25 7591

West Coast Hydroponics
662 Stirling Highway, Mosman Park WA 6012
Tel: (09) 383 4933 Fax: (09) 383 4644

Associations

Australian Hydroponics Association Inc.
12 Jikara Drive, Glen Osmond SA 5064
Tel: (08) 37 9130

Bundaberg & District Hydroponics Association
PO Box 911, Bundaberg Qld 4670
Tel: (071) 52 8448

Cairns Hydroponics Association
c/- PO Box 92, Westcourt Qld 4870
Tel: (070) 55 9813

Central Districts Hydroponics Association
Tel: (049) 47 1777

Cooloola Hydroponic Club
Mail Service 316, Gympie Qld 4570
Tel: (074) 83 3944

Darwin Hydroponics Society
PO Box 38830, Winnellie NT 0821
Tel: (089) 27 3368

Hydroponic Association of Queensland
PO Box 1291, Milton Qld 4064
Tel: (075) 37 4134

Hydroponics Society of South Australia
PO Box 134, Daw Park SA 5041
Tel: (08) 251 4016

Hydroponic Society of Victoria
PO Box 212, Monbulk Vic 3793
Tel: (03) 376 0447

Northern Rivers Hydroponic Association
PO Box 60, Murwillumbah NSW 2484
Tel: (066) 87 6707

Sydney Hydroponics Association
Lot 45 Bennett Street, Londonderry NSW 2753
Tel: (045) 72 5393

Further reading

Australian Hydroponics Association Inc., *Proceedings — South Pacific Hydroponics Conferences*, Southport, 1990.

Bridwell, Raymond, *Hydroponic Gardening*, Woodbridge Press, Santa Barbara, 1989.

Colcheedas, Tom, *Hydroponics Simplified*, Tom Colcheedas, Melbourne, 1992.

Douglas, James Sholto, *Advanced Guide to Hydroponics*, Penguin, London, 1976.

Mason, John, *Commercial Hydroponics*, Kangaroo Press, Sydney, 1990.

Resh, Howard M., *Hydroponic Food Production*, Woodbridge Press, Santa Barbara, 1989.

Resh, Howard M., *Hydroponic Home Food Gardens*, Woodbridge Press, Santa Barbara, 1990.

Romer, Joe, *Hydroponic Gardening in Australia*, Reed Books, Sydney, 1986.

Romer, Joe, *Hydroponics for Everyone*, Shepp Books, Sydney, 1985.

Smith, Denis L., *Rockwool in Horticulture*, Grower Books, London, 1987.

Sundstrom, A. C., *Simple Hydroponics*, Penguin, Melbourne, 1979.

Sutherland, Dr Struan K., *Hydroponics for Everyone*, Hyland House, Melbourne, 1987.

Van Patten, George F., *The Rockwool Book*, Van Patten Publishing, Portland, 1991.

Van Patten, George F., *Gardening Indoors*, Van Patten Publishing, Portland, 1986.

Index